THE OLD
FARMER'S ALMANAC
FOR
KIDS

VOLUME 9

YANKEE PUBLISHING INCORPORATED,
AN EMPLOYEE-OWNED COMPANY

P9-DHJ-051

The Old Farmer's Almanac Books

Publisher: Sherin Pierce
Editor in Chief: Janice Stillman
Art Director: Colleen Quinnell
Series Editor: Sarah Perreault
Managing Editor: Jack Burnett
Contributors: Kelly Alder, Derrick Barnes, Bob Berman, Emma Biggs, Christopher Burnett, Jack Burnett, Alice Cary, Tim Clark, Janet Dohner, Stephanie Gibeault, Mare-Anne Jarvela, Benjamin Kilbride, Barbara Lassonde, Martie Majoros, Sheryl Normandeau, Sarah Perreault, Heidi Stonehill, Robin Sweetser, Carol Watson

V.P., New Media and Production: Paul Belliveau
Production Director: David Ziarnowski
Production Manager: Brian Johnson
Senior Production Artists: Jennifer Freeman, Rachel Kipka, Janet Selle

Companion Web site: Almanac.com/Kids

Senior Digital Editor: Catherine Boeckmann
Associate Digital Editor: Christopher Burnett
New Media Designer: Amy O'Brien
Digital Marketing Specialist: Holly Sanderson
E-mail Marketing Specialist: Samantha Caveny
E-commerce Director: Alan Henning
Programming: Reinvented, Inc.

For additional information about this and other publications from *The Old Farmer's Almanac,* visit **Almanac.com** or call **1-800-ALMANAC (1-800-256-2622)**

Distributed in the book trade in the United States by Houghton Mifflin Harcourt and in Canada by Thomas Allen & Son Limited

Direct-to-retail and bulk sales are handled by Stacey Korpi, 800-895-9265, ext. 160

Yankee Publishing Inc., P.O. Box 520, 1121 Main Street, Dublin, New Hampshire 03444

ISBN: 978-1-57198-896-6

ISSN: 1948-061X

FIRST PRINTING OF VOLUME 9

Thank you to everyone who had a hand in producing this Almanac and getting it to market, including printers, distributors, and sales and delivery people, and thanks to all of you who bought it!

PRINTED IN THE UNITED STATES OF AMERICA

HEY, YOU!

YES, YOU!

DID YOU KNOW THAT THIS *OLD FARMER'S ALMANAC FOR KIDS* HAS ITS OWN WEB SITE?

NIGHT SKY   **JOKES & FUN**   **TIME TRAVEL**   **ANIMAL LOVERS**   **WEATHER WATCH**

That's right! Almanac.com/Kids is filled with **TONS MORE** of the same cool, quirky, awesome, and amazing stuff that you see on these pages!

Tickle your brain with the **Question of the Day**— and then share what you've learned.

Use the **Birthday Finder** to learn who shares your birthday (and your friends' birthdays, too).

 Read some **jokes** and laugh out loud!

 Check out the **weather** and find out the **Moon phase!**

Explore to find more incredible stuff! Most important, have fun!

EXPAND YOUR EXPERIENCE AT
ALMANAC.COM/KIDS

CONTENTS

8

CALENDAR

What Happened in History? 8

Why the Week Has Seven Days 20

Kindness Is Contagious! 24

ASTRONOMY

Perplexing Pluto's Planet Status 28

Behold the "Supermoon"! 31

So, You Want to Live in Space? 32

The Astronaut Who Was Allergic
to the Moon 38

32

WEATHER

Up in the Clouds 40

Weather Plot Symbols 46

Weather Tracker 47

How Cold *Was* It? 48

Nature's Weather Signs 54

ON THE FARM

Cows and Moos 56

Old MacDonald Had a Dog 64

40

IN THE GARDEN

Pots That Rock! **70**

Meet the Humble Bumble **74**

Who Put the "Straw"
in Strawberries? **78**

Garden Snack Attack **84**

Grow Trash-Can Potatoes **88**

NATURE

The Big Cats **90**

Craft Some Pinecone Critters! **96**

Make Way for Duck Stamps **98**

Dynamic Dart Frogs **102**

Eyes on the Skies for Dragonflies! . . . **108**

AWESOME ACHIEVERS

Look What I Found! **112**

Environmental Warriors **118**

CONTENTS

130

138

154

FOOD

Cracking the Coconut **126**

Breakfast Around the World **130**

Fun and Flavorful! **134**

SPORTS

Games of Glory:
All About the Olympics **138**

Frozen Football: The Ice Bowl **146**

The Pine Tar Incident **152**

HEALTH

Know Your Nose **154**

The Body Parts Rap **158**

Blood: The Good and the Gross **162**

PETS

The *Other* Washington Zoo **166**

Calming Creatures **170**

AMUSEMENT

Do You See It? 174

Amazing and True! 176

What Are You Afraid Of? 179

Sign Here 180

How a Comic Strip Is Made 182

Table of Measures 186

Solutions to Games and Puzzles 187

FUN & GAMES

The Halloween Hunt 23

Mirrored Twins 27

Travel Unravel 63

Digging for Garden Words 89

Create Your Own Colorful Frogs 106

Treasure Hunt 117

Penguin Pucks 145

Acknowledgments 188

Index 191

WHAT HAPPENED IN HISTORY?

JANUARY

1
New Year's Day

3
Spirit rover landed on Mars, 2004

5
The word "hamburger" first appeared in print, in the *Walla Walla Union*, Washington, 1889

Convert to metric on p. 186

8
New York City stayed below 0°F all day, 1859

10
Vancouver, British Columbia, had 23 consecutive days of rain, 2006

January is here,
With eyes that keenly glow—
A frost-mailed warrior striding
A shadowy steed of snow.
—Edgar Fawcett, American poet (1847–1904)

11
Sir John A. Macdonald, 1st Canadian prime minister, born, 1815

13
Mickey Mouse comic strip debuted in newspapers, 1930

15
Civil rights leader Martin Luther King Jr. born, 1929

18
A half-pound meteorite crashed through the office of Dr. Frank Ciampi in Lorton, Virginia, 2010

20
Barack Obama sworn in as 44th U.S. president, 2009

23
−73°F in Iroquois Falls, Ontario, 1935

25
President John F. Kennedy became first U.S. president to hold a live televised news conference, 1961

26
Hockey player Wayne Gretzky born, 1961

28
National Blueberry Pancake Day

31
Singer Justin Timberlake born, 1981

MOON NAME: FULL WOLF MOON

FEBRUARY

MOON NAME: FULL SNOW MOON

1
Tom Brady became youngest quarterback to lead team (New England Patriots) to two Super Bowl victories, 2004

4
Winter Olympics held in U.S. for first time, Lake Placid, New York, 1932

6
Alan Shepard became first person to hit a golf ball on the Moon, 1971

7
Basketball player Steve Nash born, 1974

8
Snow fell in Los Angeles, California, 1989

9
National Pizza Day

10
28 skiers performed back flips while holding hands, Bromont, Quebec, 1982

12
Abraham Lincoln, 16th U.S. president, born, 1809

13
First Barbie dolls went on sale, 1959

14
Valentine's Day

20
Singer Rihanna born, 1988

22
George Washington, 1st U.S. president, born, 1732

24
Pilots of two planes reported UFO over Arizona, 2018

27
Bronze sculpture of civil rights activist Rosa Parks unveiled, Washington, D.C., 2013

On the wind in February.
Snowflakes float still,
Half inclined to turn to rain,
Nipping, dripping, chill.
–Christina Rossetti, English poet (1830–94)

CALENDAR

MARCH

The stormy March is come at last,
With wind, and cloud, and
changing skies;
I hear the rushing of the blast
That through the snowy valley flies.
–William Cullen Bryant, American poet
(1794-1878)

1
Yellowstone National Park created, 1872

2
Dr. Seuss (real name: Theodor Seuss Geisel) born, 1904

3
First organized ice hockey game, Montreal, Quebec, 1875

7
Barefoot water-skier Fernando Reina Iglesias, towed by helicopter, reached speed of 153 mph, 2011

8
1.6-inch–diameter hailstone fell on Erin, Ontario, 1879

10
Singer Carrie Underwood born, 1983

12
Girl Scouts founded by Juliette Low, 1912

13
National Chicken Noodle Soup Day

14
Marc Garneau chosen as first Canadian to go into space, 1984

17
St. Patrick's Day

19
1,383-square-foot omelet made, Yokohama, Japan, 1994

24
Magician Harry Houdini born, 1874

26
−69°F in Allakaket, Alaska, 1954

27
Actress Brenda Song born, 1988

30
Jeopardy! debuted on television, 1964

MOON NAME: FULL WORM MOON

APRIL

MOON NAME: FULL PINK MOON

1
All Fools' Day

3
First mobile phone call made, 1973

5
102-year-old Elsie McLean became oldest golfer to make a hole-in-one on a regulation course, 2007

7
Toronto Blue Jays played their first American League baseball game, 1977

8
Actress Skai Jackson born, 2002

10
253-mph gust of wind recorded on Barrow Island, Australia, during Cyclone Olivia, 1996

12
Terry Fox began his "Marathon of Hope" across Canada, 1980

14
RMS *Titanic* struck an iceberg on its maiden voyage, 1912

16
Chance the Rapper born, 1993

21
13-year-old Morgan Pozgar won LG National Texting Championship, 2007

22
Earth Day

24
Singer Kelly Clarkson born, 1982

26
National Pretzel Day

30
Oklahoma City had no thunderstorms in April for first time in recorded history, 1989

Gladness is born of the April weather,
And the heart is as light as a wind-tossed feather.
Who could be sad on a day like this?
The care that vexed us no longer is.
–Eben Eugene Rexford, American poet (1848-1916)

2

MAY

The earth is waking at the voice of May,
The new grass brightens by the trodden way,
The woods wave welcome to the sweet spring day,
And the sea is growing summer blue.

–Elizabeth Akers Allen, American poet (1832–1911)

1
May Day

2
Actor Dwayne "The Rock" Johnson born, 1972

4
Royal Canadian Mint produced its last penny, 2012

5
Singer Adele born, 1988

7
Bigfoot reportedly seen in Hollis, New Hampshire, 1977

10
Christopher Columbus sighted Cayman Islands and named them Las Tortugas, 1503

12
Montreal, Quebec, chosen as site for 1976 Summer Olympics, 1970

14
Filmmaker George Lucas born, 1944

17
First Kentucky Derby held, 1875

18
Pitcher Randy Johnson (age 40) became oldest major league baseball player to throw perfect game, 2004

20
For third year in a row, Codell, Kansas, was hit by a tornado on this date, 1918

22
First permanent IMAX theater opened, Toronto, Ontario, 1971

25
Daniel Goodwin climbed Chicago's Sears Tower using suction cups, 1981

27
National Grape Popsicle Day

28
Football player Michael Oher born, 1986

31
1,376-lb. Pacific blue marlin caught, Kaiwi Point, Kona, Hawaii, 1982

MOON NAME: FULL FLOWER MOON

JUNE

MOON NAME: FULL STRAWBERRY MOON

2
Elizabeth II crowned queen of England, 1953

3
James Cameron announced as inductee into Canada Walk of Fame, 2008

6
4 inches of snow fell, Regent, North Dakota, 2009

8
Bald eagle placed under federal protection as endangered species in U.S., 1940

10
Ben Franklin's kite-and-key experiment proved lightning is electricity, 1752

12
Chicago Bulls won their first NBA championship, 1991

13
Actor Chris Evans born, 1981

14
Flag Day (U.S.)

17
Tennis player Venus Williams born, 1980

19
Garfield the Cat made his comic strip debut, 1978

21
Tallest structure built with LEGOs (114 feet 11 inches) set Guinness World Record, Milan, Italy, 2015

22
12 inches of rain fell in 42 minutes, Holt, Missouri, 1947

24
Actress Mindy Kaling born, 1979

26
National Chocolate Pudding Day

27
Bill passed making "O Canada" Canadian national anthem, 1980

30
Olympic swimmer Michael Phelps born, 1985

And since all this loveliness can not be Heaven, I know in my heart it is June.
Abba Goold Woolson, American writer
(1838–1921)

JULY

Cool in the very furnace of July
The water-meadows lie;
The green stalks of their grasses and their flowers
They still refresh at fountains never dry.
—John Drinkwater, English poet (1882–1937)

1
Canada Day

3
New Hampshire's Mount Washington Cog Railway opened to public, 1869

4
U.S. Independence Day

6
7,000+ lightning strikes lit up skies over Greater Vancouver and southern Vancouver Island, British Columbia, 1997

9
Actor Tom Hanks born, 1956

11
United Nations announced world population more than 5,000,000,000 (5 billion), 1987

12
Dwight Eisenhower became first U.S. president to fly in a helicopter, 1957

13
National French Fries Day

16
Harry Potter and the Half-Blood Prince sold 6.9 million copies in first 24 hours, 2005

17
Disneyland Park opened in Anaheim, California, 1955

22
Singer and actress Selena Gomez born, 1992

23
Largest-diameter hailstone (8 inches wide; 1 lb. 15 oz.) ever found in U.S. broke through deck, Vivian, South Dakota, 2010

24
Animal activist Bindi Irwin born, 1998

26
First Moon rock samples analyzed, Houston, Texas, 1969

29
Boston Red Sox player Bill Mueller became first player in major league history to hit grand slams from both sides of the plate in one game, 2003

MOON NAME: FULL BUCK MOON

AUGUST

MOON NAME: FULL STURGEON MOON

2
Cookies baked on vehicle's dashboard during heat wave, Bedford, New Hampshire, 2006

4
Actors Dylan and Cole Sprouse born, 1992

5
Cornerstone for pedestal of Statue of Liberty laid, 1884

7
George Washington established Badge of Military Merit for U.S. soldiers injured in action (now called Purple Heart), 1782

9
Donald Duck received a star on Hollywood Walk of Fame, 2004

10
National S'mores Day

12
Olympic speed skater Cindy Klassen born, 1979

14
Aretha Franklin inducted into Gospel Music Hall of Fame, 2012

15
Thomas Edison suggested saying "Hello" when answering phones, 1877

16
Actress Evanna Lynch born, 1991

17
The Wizard of Oz premiered on East Coast, New York City, 1939

21
Tropical Storm Fay made landfall in Florida for third time in a week, 2008

25
Chef Rachael Ray born, 1968

26
Women's Equality Day (U.S.)

29
Althea Gibson became first African-American woman to compete in a national tennis tournament, 1950

30
Streetcar service ended in Montreal, Quebec, 1959

Buttercup nodded and said good-bye,
Clover and daisy went off together,
But the fragrant water lilies lie
Yet moored in the golden August weather.
—Celia Thaxter, American poet (1835–94)

SEPTEMBER

O sweet September rain!
I hear it fall upon the garden beds,
Freshening the blossoms which begin to wane.
–Mortimer Collins, English poet (1827–76)

2
Diana Nyad completed 2-day, 2-night swim from Cuba to Florida, 2013

4
Singer Beyoncé Knowles born, 1981

5
National Cheese Pizza Day

7
Google Inc. founded, 1998

8
Rare black rhino born, Pittsburgh Zoo, Pennsylvania, 2012

11
Patriot Day (U.S.)

12
Hot, dry winds caused tree foliage to crumble, east Kansas, 1882

13
Protester dressed as Batman scaled front wall of Buckingham Palace, England, 2004

16
Actress Alexis Bledel born, 1981

18
Central Intelligence Agency (CIA) founded, 1947

20
Cal Ripken Jr. took a day off for first time in 16 years, ending his streak at 2,632 baseball games, 1998

21
The Hobbit by J.R.R. Tolkien first published, 1937

23
Time capsule buried on site of New York World's Fair, to be opened in 6939, 1938

24
Sun and Moon appeared blue/pink/purple over northeastern U.S. due to smoke from forest fires in Alberta and British Columbia, Canada, 1950

25
Actor Will Smith born, 1968

27
Jeffrey Petkovich and Peter Debernardi went over Niagara Falls in a barrel, 1989

29
Snow began to fall in Caribou, Maine, ending on the 30th, with 2.5 inches, 1991

MOON NAME: FULL CORN MOON

OCTOBER

MOON NAME: FULL HUNTER'S MOON

1
Henry Ford's Model T automobile introduced ($850 price), 1908

3
Actor Noah Schnapp born, 2004

5
Laurie Skreslet became first Canadian to summit Mt. Everest, 1982

7
First photos of dark side of Moon, 1959

8
Singer Bruno Mars born, 1985

11
U.S. president Jimmy Carter received Nobel Peace Prize, 2002

12
Columbus Day "Big Blow" in Oregon and Washington brought 100-mph winds, 1962

14
National Dessert Day

17
Ashrita Furman balanced 100 ice cream scoops on cone, 2013

19
First wedding in a balloon took place over Cincinnati, Ohio, 1874

22
Rare purple lobster caught off coast of Winter Harbor, Maine, 2019

24
Three tornadoes spurred by thunderstorms, Flagstaff, Arizona, 1992

25
Singer Katy Perry born, 1984

26
Canadian Rob Krueger became World Rock Paper Scissors champion, 2003

29
Olympic swimmer Amanda Beard born, 1981

31
All Hallows' Eve

Listen! the wind is rising, and the air is wild with leaves,
We have had our summer evenings, now for October eves!
–Humbert Wolfe, English poet (1886–1940)

NOVEMBER

The soft November days are here,
The aftermath of blossom's year.

–Sara Louisa Oberholtzer, American poet (1841–1930)

1
Montreal Canadiens player Jacques Plante became first NHL goalie to regularly use face protection, 1959

3
National Sandwich Day

5
Parker Brothers released board game *Monopoly*, 1935

7
"Galloping Gertie" bridge, Tacoma, Washington, collapsed during windstorm 4 months after grand opening, 1940

9
First documented Canadian football game played, University of Toronto, 1861

10
Sesame Street made its television debut, 1969

11
Veterans Day (U.S.), Remembrance Day (Canada)

12
Actor Ryan Gosling born, 1980

13
Ground-breaking ceremony held for Martin Luther King Jr. Memorial, Washington, D.C., 2006

16
Meteor fireball turned night into day in Finland, 2017

18
Baseball player David Ortiz born, 1975

19
U.S. president Abraham Lincoln delivered Gettysburg Address, 1863

22
Actress Scarlett Johansson born, 1984

30
Copy of Action Comics #1, famous for first appearance of Superman, sold for $2,161,000, 2011

MOON NAME: FULL BEAVER MOON

DECEMBER

MOON NAME: FULL COLD MOON

2
First pizza party in space took place on the International Space Station, 2017

4
Temperature dropped from 52°F to 18°F in 20 minutes, Livingston, Montana, 1972

5
Electric eels lit a Christmas tree at Living Planet Aquarium, Sandy, Utah, 2012

9
Marguerite d'Youville became first Canadian-born saint, 1990

10
Actress Raven-Symoné born, 1985

13
Highest-scoring game in NBA history: Detroit Pistons defeated Denver Nuggets, 186–184, 1983

16
The Tale of Peter Rabbit by Beatrix Potter first published, 1901

17
Snow fell for 3 weeks in Portland, Oregon, accumulating to 34 inches, 1884

18
Singer Billie Eilish born, 2001

21
First animated feature-length film with sound and color, *Snow White and the Seven Dwarfs*, premiered, Hollywood, California, 1937

24
"Silent Night" performed for first time, Oberndorf, Austria, 1818

25
Christmas Day

26
Powerful 9.0 earthquake erupted underwater off island of Sumatra, 2004

28
83 inches of snow reported on the ground, Bathurst, New Brunswick, 1978

29
William Lyon Mackenzie King became 10th prime minister of Canada, 1921

30
National Bacon Day

31
Olympic gymnast Gabby Douglas born, 1995

Chill December brings the sleet,
Blazing fire, and Christmas treat.
—Sara Coleridge, English poet (1802–52)

WHY THE

WEEK

The length of a year corresponds to the movement of Earth around the Sun, and the length of a month corresponds to the Moon's revolution around Earth, but what about the length of a week? It makes no astronomical sense whatsoever.

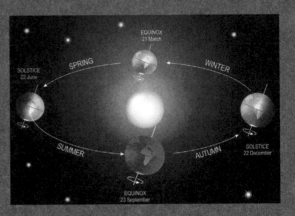

A week is roughly the length of a phase of the Moon—7 days, 9 hours. But centuries ago, as those 9 hours piled up, they caused chronographic chaos. To create order, people devised solutions.

Astrologers in Mesopotamia, one of the earliest civilizations in the Middle East, created the first 7-day week when they designated one day for each of the seven most prominent objects in the sky: the Sun, the Moon, and the five major planets visible to the naked eye.

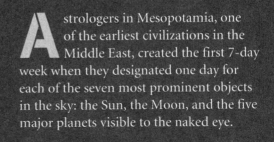

YEARS AGO, THIS WASN'T ALWAYS THE CASE. HISTORY, RELIGION, AND CULTURE HAVE ALL PLAYED A ROLE IN CREATING WHAT WE USE TODAY.

HAS

SEVEN DAYS

Early Jews also adopted a 7-day week but based it on the 6 days that it took the Lord to create the universe, as reported in the Book of Genesis in the Scriptures. We can thank them for adding the first regularly scheduled day of observance unrelated to natural phenomena—the Sabbath, or day of rest.

In some ancient societies, the market schedule determined the length of a week. In West Africa, a week was 4 days; in Assyria, 6 days; in Rome, 8; in Egypt, 10; in China, 15.

In 1793, the leaders of the French Revolution produced a calendar with three 10-day periods in each month. It never caught on.

In 1929, officials in the Soviet Union (which included Russia) invented a 5-day week based on the colors green, orange, purple, red, and yellow. Each citizen was assigned a color as his or her day off. It didn't last. In 1932, numbers replaced colors and the week was extended to 6 days. This also failed, and by 1940, Soviets were using 7 days like the rest of the world.

Mathematically, a 7-day week makes no sense, either. It doesn't divide evenly into a 365- or 366-day year, and many holidays fall on different days of the week each year. But this is what we all have become accustomed to. After all, would you want your birthday to be on the same day of the week forever?

THE HALLOWEEN HUNT

Find seven differences between the two scenes below.

(SOLUTION ON PAGE 187.)

Kindness Is Contagious!

World Kindness Day, celebrated every year on **November 13,** encourages people to show kindness toward others and do good deeds. Founded in 1998 by the World Kindness Movement, World Kindness Day is observed all over the world.

Kindness is not taught like math or spelling, with textbooks and quizzes; it is learned through real-life examples and experiences. You can show your friends, siblings, and peers how to be kind through your own actions. Even a smile or friendly "hello" can brighten someone's day. Science has proven that kindness is contagious; when you show kindness toward someone, that person is more likely to do a kind act of their own.

Here are some ideas for ways to spread kindness.

At Home:

- ○ Call your grandparents or write them a letter.
- ○ Offer to do an extra chore.
- ○ Play a game with your brother and/or sister. (Let them choose the game.)
- ○ Ask your parents how you can help to make their day easier.
- ○ Tell your parents how much you appreciate them.

At School:

- ○ At lunch, sit with someone who is alone at their table.
- ○ Tell your teacher what you like about their class.
- ○ Help to clean up the lunchroom.
- ○ Speak up if you see a student being treated badly.
- ○ Offer to help another student with their homework.

In Your Community:

- Put an elderly neighbor's trash bins on the sidewalk on collection day and return the trash bins after they are emptied.
- Do a chore for a new mother on your block.
- Donate clean towels or new pet toys to a local animal shelter.
- Bake some cookies for a family in your neighborhood.
- Rake a neighbor's lawn or shovel snow out of their driveway.

Kindness Comes Back

Did you know that being kind has a positive effect on you? The good feelings that you experience after an act of kindness release hormones called endorphins in your body. These hormones trigger the part of your brain responsible for feeling joy and happiness. Research has shown that people who regularly practice kindness have better relationships with their friends and family and also have healthier hearts!

Make kindness a habit and do something nice for someone every day. Being kind not only serves as an example for others to follow but also makes the world a better place in which to live.

Mirrored Twins

Try to find the mirrored copy for each picture.

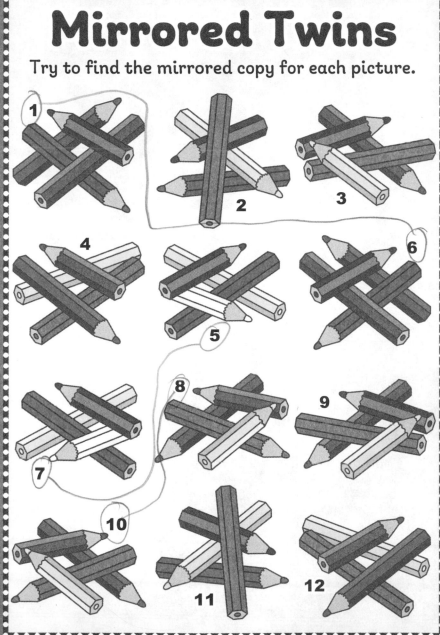

PERPLEXING
PLUTO'S
PLANET
STATUS

DO YOU KNOW PLUTO?

● Pluto has five moons: Charon, Nix, Hydra, Kerberos, and Styx. Charon, the largest, is so big that it and Pluto orbit each other.

● Pluto is small. It's only about half the width of the United States.

● One day on Pluto takes about 153 hours, and 1 year lasts 248 Earth years.

● Pluto has a frozen heart-shape area on its surface called "Tombaugh Regio" after the astronomer who discovered the dwarf planet. The heart even appears to "beat" when the ice becomes vapor during the day and freezes again at night.

ASTRONOMY

Imagine comparing photographs of the night sky and looking for any object that may have shifted position from one photo to the next. What a tedious task! Over 90 years ago, this was exactly what Clyde Tombaugh was doing at the Lowell Observatory in Arizona. He was searching for Planet X—an as-yet-undiscovered ninth planet that people mistakenly thought was influencing wobbles in the orbits of Neptune and Uranus. On the afternoon of February 18, 1930, he discovered what we now know as Pluto.

NAMED FOR A GOD OF THE UNDERWORLD

Pluto was named after the Roman god of the underworld. An 11-year-old girl in Oxford, England, chose the name. Upon hearing about the discovery, Venetia Burney said to her grandfather, "Why not call it Pluto?" Luckily for Venetia, her grandfather passed her suggestion on to some local astronomers, and it made its way to the Lowell Observatory. The stargazers at the observatory liked her suggestion, and on May 1, 1930, they announced the new name. When Venetia's grandfather heard the news, he gave her 5 pounds (like dollars in the United States) as a reward.

DEMOTION TO A DWARF PLANET

When Clyde first discovered Pluto, it was considered the ninth planet in our solar system. But as astronomers discovered more objects in space, the International Astronomical Union (IAU) decided that it was time to get precise about which bodies in space deserved the label of "planet." On August 24, 2006, the IAU announced their new definition, and Pluto didn't measure up. Instead, it became known as a dwarf planet. But Pluto isn't the only dwarf planet. There are four others: Ceres, Eris, Makemake, and Haumea.

Why was Pluto demoted? Was it because it wouldn't stop teasing Uranus and Neptune? No. And it didn't have anything to do with Pluto's extreme distance from the Sun—a whopping 3.67 billion miles, on average. In fact, Pluto meets the first two requirements of being a planet: It orbits the Sun and it is nearly round.

So, what's the problem? Pluto is simply too messy. Just like when you clean your room and either put things away or throw them out, a planet must clear all of the debris in the neighborhood around its orbit by absorbing it, causing it to orbit the planet, or pushing it farther into space. Pluto's orbit is too full of icy chunks for it to earn the title of "planet."

Although Pluto is no longer a planet, there may still be a Planet X waiting for discovery. Some astronomers at the California Institute of Technology believe that there is a possible ninth planet that would take 10,000 to 20,000 years to orbit the Sun.

ALL IN THE FAMILY

Venetia was not the first in her family to name a heavenly body. Her great-uncle, Henry Madan, had named Phobos and Deimos, the moons of Mars.

Behold the "Supermoon"!

Sometimes celestial bodies aren't what they
seem to be. Here, our astronomer,
Bob Berman, explains how the Moon's
distance from Earth can affect what
we see—or think we see.

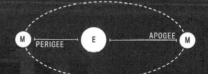

The Moon is never the same distance from Earth. This is due
to the Moon's orbit, which is not a perfect circle. Instead,
it is somewhat oval-like, or elliptical. The point at which it
is *nearest* Earth each lunar month is called its perigee. The point at
which it is *farthest* from Earth each lunar month is called its apogee.

The nearness of a full Moon at perigee causes it to appear slightly
bigger and brighter. That's why it's called a "Supermoon"!

There is another phenomenon that can make the Moon appear
larger than it really is. When the Moon is low, you see it in relation
to earthly objects, such as chimneys or trees, whose size and shape
provide scale. Your brain compares the size of the Moon to the trees,
buildings, or other reference points, and suddenly the Moon looks
massive! This effect is called the "Moon illusion."

SO, YOU WANT TO
LIVE IN SPACE?

Space living is an adventure. Take it from NASA astronaut Peggy Whitson, who has spent a record-setting 665 days in space and reports, "The space station is not really a hotel yet. I would call it a camping trip."

WHAT IT TAKES TO BECOME A NASA ASTRONAUT

Do you want to be one of the first humans to travel to Mars? In addition to having excellent leadership, teamwork, and communication skills, NASA requires an astronaut to . . .

- be a U.S. citizen
- have a master's degree in a STEM field (Science, Technology, Engineering, Mathematics) or equivalent academic or test pilot experience

- have at least 2 years of related professional experience or at least 1,000 hours of being a pilot-in-command on jet aircraft
- be able to pass a physical exam

Once selected, astronauts report to Johnson Space Center in Houston, Texas, where they spend 2 years learning to do things like walk in (simulated) space, operate the International Space Station (ISS), and control a robotic arm.

CAN'T WAIT?

Each year, the Alabama Space Science Exhibit Commission offers a variety of programs for kids ages 7 and up at Space Camp (www.spacecamp.com), on the grounds of the U.S. Space & Rocket Center in Huntsville, Alabama. There, participants learn space and flight history, complete simulated space missions, and learn what it's like to be an astronaut.

SPACE STINKS!

Astronauts aren't sure what space smells like because if they took off their helmets to sniff, they would die. But they've gotten whiffs of things that have been in space—like their space suits—and say that such things have a burnt, metallic smell. This odor may come from particles released into space during nuclear reactions from stars and supernovae.

LIGHT AS A FEATHER?

Gravity is an invisible force that pulls objects toward each other. It's what brings you back to the ground after you jump in the air and also what holds the Moon in its orbit around Earth. However, gravity becomes weaker with distance. Astronauts aboard the ISS are subject to some of Earth's gravity—but they don't feel it. The space station and everything inside it is in freefall as it orbits Earth, making astronauts and the objects inside appear to be weightless. This effect is called "microgravity." (It's also called "zero gravity," but this term is misleading.) Microgravity makes heavy objects easy to move. On the ISS, astronaut Suni Williams could easily lift a piece of equipment that weighs more than 700 pounds on Earth.

MICROGRAVITY TAKES SOME GETTING USED TO

Microgravity has many effects on the human body. Muscles and bones can become weaker because they don't have to work as hard as they do on Earth. Astronauts often feel queasy for a few days as their bodies adjust. Sometimes their sense of up and down gets confused because they can't immediately figure out where the floor and ceiling are. "The first night in space, when I was drifting off to sleep," one astronaut said, "I suddenly realized that I had lost track of . . . my arms and legs. For all my mind could tell, my limbs were not there."

Once back on Earth, astronauts may wobble or stumble for a day or so as they get used to the full force of gravity. After returning from the ISS, astronauts typically complete a 45-day "reconditioning period" with exercises designed to rebuild bone mass and muscle strength lost while in space.

WATCH WHERE (AND HOW) YOU STEP

Astronauts wear sneakers only when using exercise equipment. The rest of the time, they wear socks and hook their feet into foot rails or fabric loops when they need to stay in one place. However, these fasteners put pressure on the tops of their feet. Astronaut Scott Kelly said that the tops of his feet became as rough as alligator skin.

Meanwhile, after about 2 months in space, rough skin on the bottoms of astronauts' feet peels off, much like what happens after a sunburn. The remaining skin is soft like a baby's skin, since these feet aren't getting the daily pounding that they would typically get from walking on Earth.

HOLD YOUR HEAD HIGH—AND HIGHER

After almost a year in space, Scott Kelly returned to Earth 2 inches taller. On Earth, gravity compresses the disks in our spine; in space, they expand, making astronauts taller. After a few days or weeks on Earth, astronauts return to their original height.

SAFETY ALERT!

Watch out for stray hairs and fingernail clippings! They can be inhaled or float into an astronaut's eye. Astronauts give each other haircuts with a vacuum at the ready and clip fingernails near air ducts.

KEEP THE EYEGLASSES HANDY

Astronauts need to have excellent vision to qualify for missions, but being in space affects their sight. As one astronaut was about to return to Earth, he discovered that he couldn't read the landing checklist. (Thankfully, he knew just what to do.) Problems like this are so common that space stations keep a supply of different prescription glasses onboard.

Because of microgravity, fluid builds up around astronauts' eyes, which can flatten their eyeballs and inflame their optic nerves. Although vision usually returns to normal once the explorers return to Earth, scientists worry that a visit to Mars—which could last as long as 3 years—might seriously damage the eyesight of the astronauts on board.

WHAT'S COOKING?

Astronauts eat meals from food pouches by using Velcro, magnets, and straps to keep food and utensils from floating away. Most of the food is freeze-dried or dehydrated, but some items, such as cookies and nuts, can be eaten in their natural form. Others—like macaroni and cheese and spaghetti— need water added.

Salt and pepper come in liquid form—otherwise, they would float away, clogging air vents or going into astronauts' eyes. (Pepper is placed in oil; salt is dissolved in water.) Astronauts use bottles with droppers to add these seasonings to their food.

TASTE TESTS

Not only is space food different, but also it doesn't always taste the same. The lack of gravity increases fluids in the upper body, leaving astronauts feeling a bit stuffy and congested. This change can affect an astronaut's sense of smell and taste. As a result, many astronauts prefer spicy food— and reach for the hot sauce—because they can taste it better.

WHAT TO WEAR

The crew doesn't change clothes as often as they would on Earth. Luckily, there's deodorant, and since they don't go outside (except in space suits), they don't get very dirty. On average, they change clothes every 10 days. They change underwear and socks every other day.

ASTRONAUTS DON'T ALWAYS SMELL SO SWEET

Because the water supply is limited and water and soapsuds stick to everything, astronauts can't shower or take a bath. Instead, they take sponge baths by squeezing liquid soap and water from pouches onto their skin. They shampoo with rinseless soap and water on their hair, while an airflow system removes any leftover water.

ABOUT THAT WATER . . .

All of the water aboard the ISS is recycled—even the astronauts' breath moisture and urine—so that it can be reused. The good news is that it's all purified through filters first, a process that takes about 8 days, and astronauts say that it tastes fine.

SWEET DREAMS

Astronauts aboard the ISS sleep in their own crew cabins, which are like small closets. Inside is a sleeping bag strapped to the wall. Astronauts also keep personal items like family photos there.

The Astronaut Who Was

I t all started with a broken fender: An easy thing to fix—if you're on Earth. On the surface of the Moon? Not so easy. The place was Taurus Littro, a valley deeper than the Grand Canyon. The date was December 11, 1972, and the fender belonged to the Lunar Rover, a high-tech vehicle designed to carry *Apollo 17* astronauts Gene Cernan and Harrison "Jack" Schmitt around the lunar surface.

How did it happen?

Gene bumped into the Rover and the rock hammer he had attached to his space suit snagged the edge of the fender and broke it off. The fender was not a strong piece of metal. Its only purpose was to keep lunar dust away from the two astronauts so that they could observe their surroundings.

But astronauts are trained to improvise repairs. Gene and Jack used a couple of maps and duct tape to replace the broken part. It worked, but a lot of moondust (also called "regolith") was tossed up in the process. It dirtied up their space suits, and when they got back inside the module, they tried to clean it off. Being in microgravity, the dust clung stubbornly to the suits and to everything else it touched, including the astronauts themselves. It smelled, Jack decided, like "spent gunpowder."

Jack could feel his nose getting congested

Allergic to the Moon

and swollen, as if he were suffering from hay fever. It seemed to him that he might be allergic to the Moon! The feeling went away after a while, but Jack, being a trained scientist, understood that what had happened to him was something unusual. No one knew what inhaling moondust might do to the human body.

More research is needed to learn about the effects of moondust—and since the Apollo program ended after Gene and Jack left the Moon, American scientists have not spent much time studying the topic. Experts warn that researchers will need 100 tons of moondust for testing before the next Moon mission, Artemis, begins in 2024.

Moondust Mayhem

Meteorites, cosmic rays, and solar winds slam into the Moon, turning its rocks into powdery topsoil called "regolith." Because there's no water or wind on the Moon to toss this moondust around and grind down its edges, regolith particles are much more jagged than those of dust on Earth. Some of them are only a few microns wide. (A micron is 1/25,000 of an inch!) This means that they can easily get deep into an astronaut's lungs and stay there, which might lead to lung problems and diseases.

Up in the Clouds

Clouds form when water vapor rises, cools, and condenses. Earth's surface features plenty of water—oceans, rivers, lakes, and ponds—and our air is full of water vapor that we don't even know is there. Water vapor can rise for three different reasons:

- **It is warmed by the Sun.**
- **Cold air moves in and pushes the warm air upward.**
- **Winds blow up against mountains, forcing wind and water vapor upward.**

The method of rising determines which kinds of clouds form. When air rises over a large area, layered clouds form. When warm air rises quickly over a small area, the clouds are puffy.

WEATHER

How Much Does a Cloud Weigh?

A typical **CUMULUS CLOUD** may be a half-mile across and a half-mile deep. A cloud that size could weigh 500 tons because of all the water droplets in it. So, how do they float if they weigh so much?

Clouds are held up by wind. As rising air causes water vapor to cool and condense, a cloud is formed. The same updrafts, or air currents, that create clouds also keep the tiny water droplets in the air. These remain suspended across a large area until enough of them combine to become heavy enough to form rain. Raindrops, then, can be thought of as tiny pieces of cloud falling on you!

**THE CLOUDS—
THE ONLY BIRDS
THAT NEVER SLEEP.**
–Victor Hugo, French poet (1802–85)

Convert to metric on p. 186

Beware of Dark Clouds

Clouds that hold a lot of moisture look dark because the water droplets inside absorb light that is passing through. Light-color clouds such as **CIRRUS (1)** and **CIRROCUMULUS (2)** contain relatively little moisture. Cirrus clouds are made almost entirely of ice crystals. Clouds such as **ALTOCUMULUS (3)** are composed mostly of water droplets and may appear as gray, puffy masses.

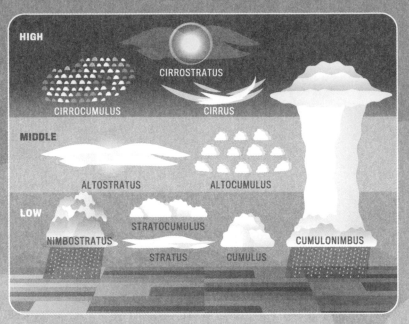

Cloud Class

HIGH CLOUDS have bases starting at about **20,000 FEET.**

CIRRUS: thin, featherlike, crystal clouds

CIRROSTRATUS: thin white clouds that resemble veils

CIRROCUMULUS: thin clouds that appear as small "cotton patches"

MIDDLE CLOUDS have bases starting at about **10,000 FEET.**

ALTOSTRATUS: a grayish or bluish layer of clouds that can obscure the Sun

ALTOCUMULUS: a gray or white layer or patches of solid clouds with rounded shapes

LOW CLOUDS have bases starting at elevations up to around **6,500 FEET.**

STRATUS: thin, gray, sheetlike clouds with a low base; may bring drizzle and snow

STRATOCUMULUS: rounded cloud masses that tend to form layers

NIMBOSTRATUS: dark, gray, shapeless cloud layers containing rain, snow, and ice pellets

CLOUDS WITH VERTICAL DEVELOPMENT form at almost any altitude and can reach up to **14,000 FEET.**

CUMULUS: fair weather clouds with flat bases and dome-shape tops

CUMULONIMBUS: large, dark, vertical clouds with bulging tops that bring showers, thunder, and lightning

Make a Cloud in a Jar

You Will Need:

1/3 CUP WARM (NOT HOT) WATER   **ICE CUBES**

WIDEMOUTH GLASS JAR WITH A LID   **HAIR SPRAY**

1. Pour warm water into the jar, then pick it up and swirl the water around.

2. Turn the lid upside-down and place it on top of the jar. Add ice cubes to fill the lid.

3. Wait 10 seconds, then quickly remove the lid and spray inside the jar with hair spray. Put the lid back in place.

4. Wait 15 seconds, remove the lid, and watch your cloud escape!

Special Clouds for Special Places

Most clouds are formed by rising air, but sinking air in thunderstorms can create sacklike forms known as MAMMATUS CLOUDS. These look ominous but are actually a sign that a thunderstorm is weakening. Mammatus, or "mammo," clouds look like upside-down pans of biscuits.

LENTICULAR CLOUDS are seen only around mountains because they are caused by mountains. These strange clouds with smooth tops and bottoms are easy to spot because they look like a stack of pancakes or flying saucers from science-fiction movies. Their most distinguishing characteristic is that they don't move. Winds blow right through them, while other clouds are swept away.

Question:

Why does it feel colder when there are no clouds?

Answer:

This is especially true in the winter. Clouds in the night sky can act like a blanket. Heat from Earth naturally rises, but the clouds hold it in place. Also, clouds in wintertime mean that the temperature is relatively mild. The air between Earth and a cloud is a bit warmer because it holds the moisture that produced the cloud in the first place.

I SAW TWO CLOUDS AT MORNING,
TINGED BY THE RISING SUN,
AND IN THE DAWN THEY FLOATED ON
AND MINGLED INTO ONE.

–John G. C. Brainard, American poet (1795–1828)

A Breath of Fresh Cloud

On a cold day, go outside and breathe out. Can you see your own breath? This is really a mini-cloud. When the warm water vapor in your breath meets cold air, it condenses onto tiny particles in the air, forming droplets. These droplets then stick together to form bigger drops that you can see.

WEATHER PLOT SYMBOLS

First developed in the 1800s, the weather plot symbols below are used to abbreviate weather data. The symbols are used by pilots, sailors, meteorologists, and people who follow the weather as a hobby. Professional weather cartographers (mapmakers) became so skilled in using these symbols that they could quickly record a location's weather in a space that could be covered by a dime! Can you think up any symbols to represent weather that you have seen? Make copies of the opposite page, track your findings, and share your observations with other weather watchers.

SKY COVERAGE

- no clouds
- one-fourth covered
- three-eighths covered
- half-covered
- five-eighths covered
- three-quarters covered
- completely overcast

HIGH CLOUDS

- cirrus
- cirrocumulus
- cirrostratus

MIDDLE CLOUDS

- altocumulus
- altostratus

LOW CLOUDS

- stratocumulus
- stratus

VERTICALLY DEVELOPED CLOUDS

- cumulus
- cumulonimbus

WEATHER CONDITIONS

- light drizzle
- steady, moderate drizzle
- steady, heavy drizzle
- light rain
- steady, moderate rain
- steady, heavy rain
- light snow
- steady, moderate snow
- steady, heavy snow
- slight hail
- freezing rain
- sleet (ice pellets)
- tornado (funnel cloud)
- dust devil
- dust storm
- fog
- heavy thunderstorm with rain
- lightning

—courtesy of U.S. National Weather Service

WEATHER TRACKER

DATE	SKY	WEATHER	DATE	SKY	WEATHER

HOW COLD WAS IT?

In an era when records for hot weather are being broken every year, cold weather is not going away.

HOW COLD WAS IT?

IT WAS SO COLD THAT WHEN I TRIED TO TAKE THE GARBAGE OUT, IT DIDN'T WANT TO GO!

Convert to metric on p. 186

Great Balls of Ice

It happens just about every winter in the Great Lakes: Ice along the shores breaks off in small pieces that, as they tumble in the waves, are rounded into "ice balls" ranging in weight from 3 to 50 pounds. Similar invasions have taken place in Alaska, Finland, and Siberia, where the "ice eggs" may be 3 feet in diameter.

Ghost Apples

Farmers who grow apples in North America have to work all year, even in winter. But they get to enjoy sights of weird beauty, such as "ghost apples"– perfectly clear, apple-shape ice balls hanging from the trees.

Susan Brown, a professor of agriculture at Cornell University, explains that when some apples are left on the tree after harvest, their flesh rots away, leaving something like applesauce inside the unbroken skin. If an ice storm should occur, coating the skin, the rotten apple drips out through the bottom, leaving behind a perfect transparent mold of the fruit until temperatures rise to melt it. She says that the phenomenon is most often found in orchards that grow Jonagold and Golden Delicious apples.

Snow Show

For a few hours on January 17 and 18, 2018, there was snow on the ground in all 50 U.S. states. The last time this happened had been in 2010. The least likely state to have snow is Florida, but its northwest corner was brushed by Winter Storm Inga. Even Hawaii usually has some snow on top of its volcano, Mauna Kea.

MAKE SOME "FRUBBLES"!

On a very cold day, get some bubble solution, go outside, and blow some frozen bubbles—or "frubbles"—by catching bubbles on your bubble wand and then watching them freeze. For best results, choose a day as close to freezing (32°F/0°C) as possible—or even below it!

HOW COLD WAS IT?
IT WAS SO COLD THAT I CHIPPED A TOOTH ON MY SOUP!

Pancake Ice . . .

Pancake, or lily pad, ice, so called because it's round in shape and has little raised ridges around its edges, can be found in both fresh and salt water. It forms wherever water that is beginning to freeze is disturbed by wind or waves. As each small chunk of ice bumps into its neighbors, a ridge begins to form, and any sharp angles on its sides are worn away. The circles can grow as large as 10 feet in diameter where conditions are right, but they never get more than a few inches thick. As the water temperatures get lower, the pancakes get stuck together and form a solid sheet.

. . . and Pancaked Tires

Drivers in very cold climates know that they need to keep their engine blocks warm with plug-in heaters so that their cars will start in frigid temperatures. But they also have problems with their tires when deep winter arrives. The air inside the tires loses about 1 pound of pressure for every 10-degree F drop in the temperature. The result? Square tires! Well, it's really just the side of the tire resting on a hard surface that flattens a little, and it gets round again once the car starts moving. But when it's really cold out—say, −30°F—getting going takes a while longer, and it's a bumpy ride!

HOW COLD WAS IT?
IT WAS SO COLD THAT WHEN WE MILKED THE COWS, WE GOT ICE CREAM!

Hot Tracks

In Chicago, when the weather gets really cold, the commuter train tracks get hot! This is because the Metra commuter rail system ignites flaming gas-fed heaters that run beside some parts of the rails. In extreme cold, metal rails and switch points can contract, leaving dangerous gaps. Warming them up closes the gaps. Maintenance workers on 12-hour shifts keep careful watch on the fires so that they don't spread beyond the heaters.

Dropping Iguanas Alert!

Temperatures below 50°F are bad news for Florida iguanas. The invasive reptiles, which can grow as long as 5 feet and weigh up to 20 pounds, are cold-blooded. When the temperature gets too low, they go into a dormant state, which may cause them to fall out of trees. They wake up when the temperature rises.

Rock-a-bye, Iggy,
In the treetops.
Better watch out
When the
*   temperature drops!*

If it goes down
Below 50 degrees,
Iguanas will tumble
Out of the trees.

Ice Volcanoes

When the temperature on the shores of the Great Lakes is slightly below freezing and the waves are several feet high, the conditions are ripe for ice volcanoes. What looks like a hill of snow on the lake surface turns out to be a hardened hollow cone of ice and snow. When the waves build up under it, it can blow its top, spewing not lava but a mix of ice and water into the air.

Cryovolcanoes, as scientists have named them, can be as small as 3 feet high or as big as a house. Hundreds of them have been known to appear around the lakes, attracting thousands of tourists—and snowy owls! The owls aren't there to see the eruptions, though. They perch on top of the cryovolcanoes to spot and dine on waterfowl swimming in the lakes.

FROZEN IN TIME

- Coldest recorded temperature on Earth: August 10, 2010, −135.8°F (East Antarctic Plateau, Antarctica)
- Coldest day in the U.S.: January 23, 1971, −80°F (Prospect Creek, Alaska)
- Coldest day in Canada: February 3, 1947, −81.4°F (Snag, Yukon)
- Fastest temperature drop: January 10, 1911, 47 degrees F in 15 minutes (Rapid City, South Dakota)
- Coldest place in the Solar System: a permanently shaded crater near the Moon's North Pole, at −415°F
- Coldest temperature in the known universe: −454.76°F in deep space outside our Solar System
- Coldest temperature theoretically possible: Absolute zero, when molecular activity ceases (−459.67°F).
- Coldest continuously inhabited place on Earth: Oymyakon, Russia, also known as "The Pole of Cold." Its record low temperature of −96°F was recorded in 1924.

NATURE'S
WEATHER SIGNS

Long before satellites and radar, people often looked to insects and other animals to predict the weather.

IF BEES FLY AWAY, FINE WILL BE THE DAY.

Fall bugs begin to chirp 6 weeks before the first frost.

When scorpions crawl, expect dry weather.

AN OPEN ANTHOLE SIGNALS CLEAR WEATHER; A CLOSED ONE, AN APPROACHING STORM.

When squirrels eat nuts on the tree, Weather as warm as warm can be.

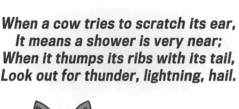

When a cow tries to scratch its ear,
It means a shower is very near;
When it thumps its ribs with its tail,
Look out for thunder, lightning, hail.

When foxes bark and utter high-pitch cries, expect strong wind and rain within 3 days.

If toads hurry toward water, it is going to thunder.

HORSES AND MULES, IF VERY LIVELY WITHOUT APPARENT CAUSE, MEANS COLD.

Hornets build nests high before warm summers and low before cold and early winters.

If sheep feed uphill in the morning, it is a sign of fine weather.

A cat sitting with its back to the fire indicates snow.

WHAT DO YOU CALL A
COW EATING GRASS?
A LAWN MOOER

Cows and Moos

The cow is of the Bovine ilk;
One end is moo, the other, milk.
–OGDEN NASH, AMERICAN POET (1902-71)

Meet the Family

- Female cattle that have given birth are called "cows."
- Female cattle that have not had a baby yet are called "heifers."
- Male cattle are called "bulls."
- Baby cattle are called "calves."

WHAT DO YOU CALL A COW WHO PLAYS THE PIANO?

A MOOSICIAN

Black, White, and Brown

In North America, there are two major types of dairy cows, or cows that give milk: Holsteins and Jerseys. Holsteins are black and white and give a lot of milk. An average Holstein produces about 24,300 pounds of milk a year. Jerseys are brown and give less milk, but the milk contains more milk fat (4.57 percent). An average Jersey produces about 17,000 pounds of milk per year. A dairy cow usually lives to be 10 to 12 years old.

MORE ABOUT MILK

- A cow must have a calf before it can produce milk.
- The average cow is 2 years old when she has her first calf.
- Cows are milked for an average of 3 to 4 years.
- Before milking machines were invented in the late 1800s, a farmer could milk only about six cows per hour. Today the farmer uses machines to milk more than 100 cows per hour!
- One average cow can give about 8 gallons of milk each day.
- A study has found that if a cow has a name, it will be less stressed and produce up to 5 percent more milk.

Convert to metric on p. 186

A "Moo Moo" Here and a "Moo Moo" There

Cows are social animals. A recent study shows that they can express their emotions to each other with different moos. They can communicate excitement and distress with individual high- or low-frequency calls.

Cows, calves, and bulls have different moos:

- A cow that is talking to its calf will use a short, soft moo to encourage the calf to get up and nurse.
- A cow that is looking for its calf will call loud and long. A cow and its calf recognize each other's moos.
- When a calf is scared or surprised, its startled moo will bring Mom running to its side.
- Bulls often moo loudly and deeply. If they see an unfamiliar bull or cow, they will moo deeply with their head held in an aggressive position.

> I never saw a Purple Cow,
> I never hope to see one;
> But I can tell you, anyhow,
> I'd rather see than be one!
> —GELETT BURGESS, AMERICAN POET AND HUMORIST (1866-1951)

Stomach Secrets

Cows have a complex stomach with four chambers. The digestion process starts when fresh grass, hay, and seeds are mixed with saliva in the mouth before being swallowed. A cow produces from 10 to 45 gallons of saliva per day, depending on the feed that it eats!

The food first goes to the biggest chamber, called the rumen, which can hold about 40 to 50 gallons of food. When this chamber is full, the food passes to the second, smaller chamber, where digestive juices ferment the food and turn it into small balls. Cows then burp up these small balls, called "cud." A cow grinds the cud in its mouth for hours. Then it swallows the food a second time, sending it back through the first two chambers and into a third chamber, where bacteria break it down. Finally, the "food" goes to the fourth chamber, where it is digested.

• A cow eats around 50 pounds of food a day and drinks about a bathtubful of water.

• A 1,000-pound cow poops about 15 times a day and produces about 10 tons of manure per year.

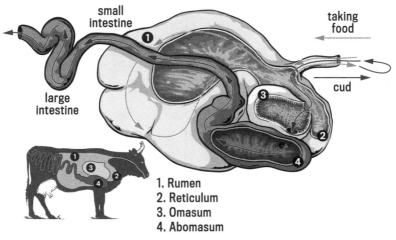

small intestine

taking food

cud

large intestine

1. Rumen
2. Reticulum
3. Omasum
4. Abomasum

COW COUNTRY

- Colorado has many geographical areas named after cows. There are 12 creeks with cow-themed names, 6 canyons, 4 gulches, and 2 lakes.
- Cow towns: Cowlic, Arizona; Concow, California; Cow Island, Louisiana; Cowpens, South Carolina
- California has the most milk cows in the United States.
- Some states, such as South Dakota, Nebraska, and Montana, have more cows than people.
- Quebec is the number one dairy cow province in Canada, with about 364,800 cows. With about 321,900, Ontario comes in second.
- Canada has about 12,500 dairy farms and almost 1 million cows.

COW LORE

According to weather lore:
- Heavy thunder will turn milk sour.
- If a cow stands with its tail to the west, the weather is said to be fair.
- If a cow stretches out its neck and sniffs the air, expect rain.

Curious Cow Facts

- Cows can sleep while they are standing!
- Cows have great senses. They can see in color and can smell things up to 6 miles away. They can hear lower and higher frequencies better than humans.
- Cows have 32 teeth but no upper front teeth.
- There are an estimated 920 breeds of cows in the world.
- Old cows in India live in cow nursing homes.

Big Bertha

Blosom

FAMOUS COWS

- Beecher Arlinda Ellen: She produced a record 5,392.7 gallons of milk in a year.
- Big Bertha, the oldest cow on record, was 48 years and 9 months old when she died in 1993. She lived in Blackwatersbridge, Ireland.
- Blosom: The world's tallest cow (over 6 feet) was a Holstein. She lived in Orangeville, Illinois, and had a misspelled name ("blossom").
- Elm Farm Ollie: In 1930, she became the first cow to fly in an airplane.
- Little Witch: The world's fastest race cow; in 2004, she ran a mile in 9 minutes, 18 seconds.
- Missy: The world's most expensive cow was sold for $1.2 million at an auction in Toronto, Ontario, in the fall of 2009.

Cow Quiz

Match each cow-related phrase with its meaning:

1. To take the bull by the horns ____

2. Holy cow! ____

3. 'Til the cows come home ____

4. A cash cow ____

5. A bull in a china shop ____

a. A very clumsy person
b. To take action right away
c. Until very late or a long time
d. A product or service that makes a lot of money
e. An expression of surprise or astonishment

KNOCK, KNOCK.
WHO'S THERE?
MOO.
MOO, WHO?
MAKE UP YOUR MIND: ARE YOU A COW OR AN OWL?

Answers: 1. b.; 2. e.; 3. c.; 4. d.; 5. a.

TRAVEL UNRAVEL

Can you find these items in the picture?

(SOLUTION ON PAGE 187.)

Red Border Collie

Old MacDonald Had a Dog

Dogs have lived with humans longer than any other animal. As the first domesticated animal, dogs protected their people, helped them to hunt for food, and carried cargo. With the development of farms, dogs got new jobs.

Dog Star
GREAT PYRENEES

This big white dog is the most famous livestock guardian. In the Pyrenees Mountains of France and Spain, shepherds have used these dogs for hundreds of years. Although they are kind, gentle giants with children and baby animals, they are extremely protective when their charges are threatened.

Other well-known livestock guardian dogs include the rugged Anatolian shepherd, ancient Italian Maremma, dreadlocked Komondor, and Turkish Akbash and Kangal dogs.

Italian Maremma

On Guard

Livestock guardian dog breeds were developed in ancient times to protect sheep, goats, and cattle from wild predators or other threats. They live with the animals that they are guarding and travel with their flocks when moving to new pastures. They have large, strong bodies and double coats that protect them from both hot and cold weather.

Livestock guardian dog breeds are gentle and devoted to their animals and family but will bark fiercely and chase off all threats. They behave independently, which means that they do not require commands or play fetch. Although they are big dogs, they resemble overgrown puppies with fluffy coats, droopy ears, and curling tails. These features make them look like a friend (and not like a wolf) to sheep and goats. Often, these breeds are the same color as their herds—white, tan, or colored in large patches.

If they do not have animals to guard, these breeds will protect their family and property. They need lots of space and good fences to be kept safely at home.

Herd Much?

In some areas, shepherds began to use a second kind of dog with their flocks. Smaller herding dogs were selected to move sheep and other animals. They use their hunting skills to chase down other animals, but they follow the shepherd's commands to control the sheep and not harm them.

Different breeds of herding dogs have different styles of herding, depending on what is needed. Fetching dogs run out and gather sheep, bringing them back to their home. Droving dogs guide animals across the countryside or on a road. Heading dogs can turn sheep or cattle around or keep them together in a group. Tending dogs pace back and forth along an imaginary line, keeping their sheep out of a road or a crop field.

Herding dogs come in different sizes, colors, and coats. They have lots of energy and need to work or play every day. They are very smart, can learn many commands, and like to chase and run.

Dog Star
BORDER COLLIE

The border collie is the most famous herding dog breed. These are medium-size dogs that come in many colors, usually with white markings on their fur. They are very intelligent and like to work for their owners.

Other herding dog breeds include the beautiful Rough collie, noble German shepherd, happy Pembroke corgi, and active Australian shepherd.

German Shepherd

Dog Star
CAIRN TERRIER

This cheerful Scottish terrier got its name from its love of hunting for prey among rock piles, or cairns, rather than digging in dirt burrows. Unlike most earthdogs, cairn terriers usually get along fine with pet dogs, and they are clever and playful companions.

Other dogs for hunting pests include the energetic Jack Russell terrier, friendly rat terrier, long-body dachshund, and bearded miniature schnauzer.

Rat Terrier

Happy Hunters

When people began farming, they required dogs to protect their stored food and crops from animal pests. These hunting dogs needed to be small enough to fit into holes, burrows, and tunnels. They also had to be brave and bold. These breeds, called earthdogs, are welcome around a barn. They also hunt small predators that bother poultry, such as foxes and weasels.

For ease in digging, their legs are short but strong. They have fur of varying colors, and their coats can be short or long. Because they are feisty and bossy, some tough earthdogs do not get along with other dogs.

Earthdogs are confident, active, and high-energy. They like to be busy and enjoy hunting and chasing small animals, so they might not get along with family pets.

Master Multitaskers

Multipurpose dogs can do several things around the farm but do not specialize in herding, guarding livestock, or hunting pests. They can work as watchdogs and chase away small predators. They help farmers to move livestock in the barnyard or keep them together on the road.

Before the invention of railroads and trucks, many of the larger breeds also had the important job of pulling small carts. In many places, they hauled firewood or supplies and took milk and other products to market.

Multipurpose dogs are the most varied in appearance and behavior. These breeds can be any size, depending on a farmer's needs. In hot places, a short coat is helpful; mountain breeds have warm, double coats for the cooler temperatures in which they live. Many multitaskers have distinctive colors and color patterns that help to identify their breed. They range from being very energetic, with a strong chase or protection drive, to being laid back and friendly with strangers.

Dog Star
NEWFOUNDLAND

Developed in Canada, Newfoundland dogs are related both to retriever hunting breeds and to fishing breeds that helped fishermen to haul in their nets, pull rope lines from boats to shore, and even rescue people who fell overboard. The sweet-tempered, giant Newfie is famous around the world for its lifesaving abilities—the breed has rescued hundreds of people from the ocean!

Other multipurpose dogs include the protective rottweiler, gentle Bernese mountain dog, sturdy Greater Swiss mountain dog, and friendly Leonberger.

Leonbergers

Pots That Rock!

Emma Biggs began helping her dad in the garden at their Toronto home at a young age. She started by watering plants and later helped to plant seeds, too. When Emma was in grade 1, she gave a presentation about gardening to the students in her school. At age 13, with help from her dad, Emma wrote a book, *Gardening With Emma.* Here, she kindly shares one of the projects from her book.

Hypertufa looks like concrete, but it is much lighter and can take a knock. I think that hypertufa looks nicer than plastic.

Making your own hypertufa pots is a fun project that you can do over the winter. Concrete is made with cement, sand, and gravel. When you make hypertufa, you change the recipe and use light ingredients such as peat moss instead of the sand and gravel, which gives you something that looks a bit like concrete or stone but is lighter.

Other common ingredients are things that you find in potting soils, like perlite and vermiculite. If you search online, you will find tons of

recipes. I like this recipe because it is really easy—I just mix cement with the potting soil!

An easy way to make hypertufa containers is to use two pots. Use the larger pot for the outside form and the smaller pot for the inside. *(continued)*

IN THE GARDEN

Hypertufa How-To

You Will Need:

2 clean plastic pots, one small enough to fit inside the other

cooking spray (or some cooking oil and an old paintbrush)

large container and tools for mixing (*I used our old wheelbarrow and a couple of shovels.*)

bucket or other container for measuring

trowel

1 part peat-based potting soil (*The potting soil I used also had perlite, which looks like little white balls. It's actually bits of volcanic rock!*)

1 part Portland cement (a common type of cement used to make concrete)

rubber gloves (*NOTE: Wet cement irritates the skin, so you will need to wear these!*)

water

1. Spray the parts of the pots that the hypertufa will touch with cooking spray (or brush with cooking oil). This prevents sticking and makes it easier to slide the molded hypertufa out of the pots once it is dry. Mix together the potting soil and Portland cement.

2. Add enough water to make the mixture completely wet but not soupy. Put about 1 inch of hypertufa at the bottom of the larger pot. This makes the bottom of your hypertufa pot.

3. Put the smaller pot on top of the layer of hypertufa and center it so that there is an equal space all around the sides. Now use a trowel to start filling up that space with your hypertufa mix, adding a bit at a time. Pack it down so that you eliminate air pockets, but don't pack it down too much, or the mix will be too dense.

4. Fill to the top of the pots and smooth out the edge. Cover the whole setup with a sheet of plastic and put it in a dry, shady spot.

Wash the container and tools that you used to mix your hypertufa quickly, before it dries onto them.

5. Let the hypertufa sit in the pots for at least a week. It will feel hard after a day or two, but it gets stronger the longer it sits and the color gets a bit lighter. When it's ready, peel the inner pot away from the sides and pull it out.

6. Turn the larger pot over and push gently from the bottom. Your new hypertufa pot should slide right out! Drill a hole in the bottom for drainage, and you are all set to plant!

MEET THE Humble

Want bumblebees to visit your garden?

There are about 46 species of bumblebees in North America alone. These large bees are round and fuzzy with short, stubby wings. You have to wonder how these big round bees fly so well. Bumblebees flap their wings back and forth rather than up and down and beat them more than 130 times per second!

Aerodynamically, the bumblebee shouldn't be able to fly, but the bumblebee doesn't know it, so it goes on flying anyway.

–Mary Kay Ash, American businesswoman (1916–2001)

Bumble

The correct answer is "Yes!" Here's why.

TOPS IN CROPS

Bumblebees are excellent pollinators—in fact, without them, a lot of food wouldn't even be able to grow! More than half of the world's crop species depend on animals to transfer pollen between male and female flower parts and thus produce fruit (even if it's a vegetable). Plants like cucumbers, peppers, tomatoes, strawberries, blueberries, raspberries, melons, and squash all benefit from bumblebees' persistent pursuit to pollinate.

Female worker bees collect the nectar and pollen. They perform a unique service called "buzz pollination" by grabbing the pollen-producing part of the plant in their jaws and vibrating their wing muscles to loosen trapped pollen. If you look closely at a bumblebee, you'll notice the pollen basket—called a "corbicula"—on its rear legs, where it stashes a load of pollen to carry back to the nest. Crops such as tomatoes, peppers, berries, and cranberries bear better fruit if they are buzz-pollinated. The flowers on berry plants are enclosed, so it takes a bumblebee's long tongue to get to the plant's nectar.

PLANT A BUMBLEBEE BUFFET

Bumblebees are not fussy; they like anything that produces nectar and pollen. If you plant even a small area or a few containers with flowering plants, the bees will find them. These fuzzy friends especially like bright-color blooms in hues of blue, purple, yellow, and white. Here are some seasonal suggestions for attracting bumblebees to your yard:

For spring, plant crocuses, Virginia bluebells, lungwort, hellebore, California poppies, and spring ephemerals.

For early and late summer, plant coneflowers, sunflowers, black-eyed Susans, bee balm, larkspur, and tall phlox.

For fall (when it gets harder to find nectar), plant salvia, wild geranium, basil, chives, cilantro, and parsley.

Q: **What do you get when you cross a bumblebee with a doorbell?**
A: **A humdinger.**

**Q: What do bumblebees chew?
A: Bumblegum.**

BEE-ING READY FOR TAKEOFF

Have you ever noticed how bumblebees just "bumble around" in the early morning, moving slowly? Their teddy bear fur and ability to regulate their body temperature allow them to be out and about on cold mornings, but they can't fly until they have warmed up.

DON'T BOTHER!

Bumblebees are the largest and gentlest of bees. They are generally very tame, and although they are able to sting, they rarely do. They do not form swarms like other communal bees, and they only sting when truly provoked. A bumblebee will even warn you before it stings. It will stick up a middle leg if it's annoyed by your presence, which means "Back off!"

THE INSIDE BUZZ
Bumblebees . . .
- are covered in an oil that makes them waterproof.
- can't see the color red.
- scent-mark flowers that they have already visited.
- can harvest pollen from flowers 400 times faster than honeybees can.
- do not make honey.

WHO PUT THE "STRAW" IN STRAWBERRIES?

Theories abound about how the strawberry got its name. One belief is that pickers used to sell small wild strawberries strung together on pieces of straw. Others think that the surface of the fruit looks like it is embedded with bits of straw. Still others say that the name comes from the Old English word meaning "to strew," because the plant's many runners (long, dangly stems) grow in all directions and look like they have been strewn (scattered) on the ground.

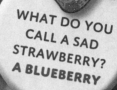

WHAT DO YOU CALL A SAD STRAWBERRY? A BLUEBERRY

WHY DID THE STRAWBERRY GO OUT WITH A FIG? BECAUSE HE COULDN'T FIND A DATE

GROW SOME
STRAWBERRIES

In the spring, check your local garden center for strawberry seedlings. Choose a sunny spot for your berries—they will need 6 to 10 hours of sun per day. If you don't have a sunny spot for planting in the ground, you can grow your strawberries in a special strawberry jar or any large container at least 10 inches in diameter and 8 inches deep.

- Plant seedlings about 20 inches apart to leave room for runners.

- Water your plants often to keep the soil moist but not water-logged. Give them extra water when the plants start growing fruit.

- If you see any weeds growing around your berries, pull them out.

- Fruit is typically ready for harvest 4 to 6 weeks after blossoming. Pick only fully red (ripe) berries, and pick every 2 to 3 days.

To have more strawberry plants, save the baby plants that grow at the end of the runners. Make sure that they have good contact with the soil. After the babies have developed roots and a few new leaves, separate them from the runner and plant them in a different area or container.

Protect your berries from berry-loving birds by spreading netting over your plants.

Most strawberry plants will grow back in the following spring if covered with mulch such as pine straw (aka pine needles) or regular straw during the cold winter months. Remove the mulch in the spring when there are no more frosty mornings.

IN THE GARDEN

SUPER
STRAWBERRIES

Strawberries are a great source of fiber and packed with vitamin C. One cup of fresh sliced berries contains more vitamin C than the recommended dietary allowance (RDA) per day. Vitamin C also is an antioxidant, which means that it helps to strengthen your immune system and give you healthy skin.

THAT'S A FACT!

- There are more than 600 varieties of strawberries.

- Strawberries are a member of the rose family.

- Strawberries are grown everywhere in North America. California produces more than 1 billion pounds a year!

- One medium strawberry has about 200 seeds.

BERRY COLORFUL

Did you know that strawberries can be other colors besides red? Look for white, purple, and yellow strawberries at the garden center or through mail order.

- 'White Soul' produces small white to cream-color berries.
- 'Purple Wonder' yields extra sweet and delicious purple fruit.
- 'Yellow Wonder' has a pleasant aroma and flavorful yellow fruit.

STRAWBERRY LEMONADE

You Will Need:

blender or food processor
bowl
wooden spoon
ice
pitcher
1 cup sliced strawberries
½ cup sugar
1 cup fresh lemon juice
1½ cups cold sparkling water

Convert to metric on p. 186

1. Ask an adult for help with putting the strawberries into the blender or food processor and puréeing them.

2. In the bowl, combine the sugar and lemon juice and stir to blend.

3. Add the sweetened lemon juice and sparkling water to the puréed berries. Process for 2 to 3 seconds to blend and then pour into an ice-filled pitcher.
Makes 3 servings.

STRAWBERRY BATH, ANYONE?

Madame Tallien, an important person at the court of French emperor Napoleon Bonaparte in the early 1800s, was famous for bathing in fresh strawberry juice. She used 22 pounds of berries per bath!

WHAT IS A SCARECROW'S FAVORITE FRUIT?
STRAW-BERRIES

SUNBURN SOOTHER

Strawberries can help to ease the discomfort of sun-damaged skin. Cut a large strawberry in half. Rub the cut side of the berry all over the sunburned area. After a few minutes, rinse the area with warm water and carefully pat your skin dry with a soft towel.

FACIAL TREAT

This strawberries-and-cream face mask will make your skin glow. It is especially helpful in the winter when your skin may be dry.

Crush three strawberries with a fork. Mix in 1 tablespoon of heavy cream and 1 teaspoon of honey. Smear the mixture on your face, avoiding your eyebrows and hairline. Leave the mixture on until it starts to dry. Rinse it off with warm water and pat your skin dry with a soft towel.

SMILE JUICE

Strawberry juice and crushed strawberries are both used to whiten discolored teeth by removing plaque and surface debris. You can try this by mixing several crushed fresh strawberries with 1 tablespoon of baking soda. Using a soft toothbrush, spread the mixture onto your teeth. Leave on for 5 minutes and then rinse with warm water. Follow up by brushing with toothpaste to remove any strawberry mixture left in your mouth. Do not use this method more than once a week, however, because the acid in strawberries may break down your enamel over time.

Note: Do not try the above remedies if you are allergic to strawberries.

GARDEN SNACK ATTACK

To have fresh, nutritious snacks at your fingertips, grow your own. Plant a snack garden!

GREEN GOODNESS

Sugar snap peas are easy to grow, can be planted early, and are among the first vegetables to be harvested from the garden. A cross between English peas and snow peas, they can be eaten pod and all—making them one of nature's healthiest fast foods. 'Sugar Snap' and 'Super Sugar Snap' are particularly sweet varieties that grow to about 5 feet tall and require some support to grow up.

Snow peas are also perfect garden snacks. Small varieties like 'Oregon Sugar Pod' will grow to about 2½ feet tall. The pods should be picked while they are still flat, before the peas get too big in the pods. Pick every 2 to 3 days to encourage more peas to grow.

HISTORICAL PEAS
The oldest pea ever discovered was found at the border of Thailand and Burma (now Myanmar). It was at least 3,000 years old!

TRIED THESE TASTY TREATS?
Ground cherries have a unique sweet tart flavor. Some have described the taste as a combination of pineapple, green grapes, and strawberries.

HIDDEN TREASURES

Have you heard of ground cherries? They are a low-growing relative of the tomato and tomatillo. Like tomatillos, ground cherries have a papery, straw-color husk, which is peeled off before eating—like opening a little present! These 1- to 3-foot-tall mini plants grow well anywhere, even in poor or sandy soil, and they keep on growing year after year. The bushes may spread up to 2 feet in diameter. Try planting 'Goldie', which produces ½- to ¾-inch yellow-orange fruit. You can snack on them fresh from the plant, made into pies and jams, or dried like raisins.

THE "OTHER" BEANS

Native to China, edamame (fresh soybean) was introduced to North America in the early 1900s. Today, it is a common snack food.

Its easy-to-grow, 2-foot-tall bushes produce mounds of pods on branches that grow from the main stem. Plant the seeds in a place that gets lots of sun. They will do well in most types of soil. When plants are about 6 inches tall, add a layer of mulch around them, up to within 1 inch of the stem. The pods are ready to be harvested when they turn dark green and the beans can just be seen in the pod. Try 'Korean Black' for its unusual appearance—the gray-black seed coats contrast with the lime green beans inside.

This snack requires some preparation: The pods need to be cooked before the beans can be eaten. Pick the pods, wash, steam for 5 to 7 minutes, drain, and sprinkle with a little salt (or not). To eat them, place the whole pod in your mouth, use your teeth to squeeze out the beans, and discard the pod.

DO YOU SPEAK JAPANESE?
When translated into English, *edamame* (ed-ah-MAH-may) means "beans on branches."

SUNFLOWER SEED FEAST

In 2001, a sunflower with 837 heads was grown by Melvin Hemker on his farm in St. Charles, Michigan.

SUNNY SEEDS

Do you like to eat sunflower seeds? They are produced on the easiest flowers to grow!

There are some sunflowers noted especially for their seed production, with whirls of tightly packed seeds that make delicious snacks. 'Mammoth Russian' forms large, yellow flowers on 10-foot-tall stems. 'Grey Stripe' is another tall choice that produces an abundance of seeds.

Plant sunflower seeds outdoors in well-drained, fertile soil. You will be able to enjoy the beautiful blooms before it is time to get the seeds for snacking.

When the back of the flower turns brown, the head starts to curl, and the petals begin to fall, it is time to harvest the seeds. Cut off the heads and hang them in an airy spot until the seeds are thoroughly dry. To release the seeds, place a bag over the flower head and shake the head gently, catching the seeds in the bag. The seeds can be roasted and then shelled for eating or shelled and eaten raw.

Grow Trash-Can Potatoes

You don't need a field or a farm to grow your own potatoes—you can grow tasty tubers in a clean plastic trash can! It's true—and here's how to do it:

YOU WILL NEED:
clean trash can
knife
ruler
garden soil
compost (optional)
seed potatoes*

Do not confuse seed potatoes with potato seeds or grocery produce! Seed potatoes are simply cut up pieces of potato with protruding eyes, or buds, that have not been chemically treated. You can find seed potatoes at local nurseries or use potatoes that were grown in your own or someone else's garden.

1. Turn the trash can upside down and ask an adult to help you cut some drainage holes in the bottom.

2. Fill the can with about 6 inches of garden soil.

3. Mix some compost into the garden soil if you have it.

4. Put the seed potatoes into the can and cover them with about 3 inches of garden soil.

5. When the plants are about 7 inches tall, add 3 to 4 more inches of soil, leaving a few inches of the plants exposed. Continue adding soil as they grow, until you fill the trash can.

6. About 3 weeks after the first flowers appear, check your crop for "new potatoes" (this is the name for potatoes harvested early); they will be under the soil. Be gentle around the roots of each plant.

7. For larger potatoes, wait until the leaves wilt and die.

8. Turn your trash can on its side and shake out your potatoes!

Potatoes need lots of water. Keep the soil moist from the time the plants appear until they bloom.

DIGGING FOR GARDEN WORDS

BOOTS   SEEDS   BUCKET   FLOWERS   HIVE   SHOVEL

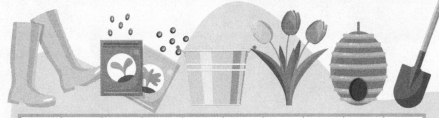

Z	W	E	P	S	H	O	V	E	L
Q	B	E	V	I	N	H	Q	O	F
M	U	I	R	F	E	N	C	E	S
M	C	H	I	V	E	W	P	Z	W
H	K	R	K	G	Y	A	Q	Y	G
E	E	S	E	E	D	S	B	F	S
Q	T	J	A	O	U	T	H	X	Z
F	L	O	W	E	R	S	O	R	M
D	B	V	B	O	O	T	S	B	E
W	B	H	Q	N	Y	F	M	P	N

(SOLUTION ON PAGE 187.)

You've seen them online, on television, and in books and movies. You may have even seen them up close in animal parks. They are huge—in size, power, and voice. What are they? They're . . .

THE BIG CATS

NATURE

HOW BIG?

The lion may be called King of the Jungle, but the largest natural big cat found in the wild is the SIBERIAN TIGER, which measures about 10.75 feet long and weighs around 660 pounds.

WHAT'S BIG? WHAT'S NOT?

The term "big cats" doesn't describe just any large wild cat. According to one definition, "big cats" all must share certain traits. Jaguars, leopards, lions, tigers, and snow leopards are big cats. "Small cats" include **COUGARS**, **CHEETAHS**, and **HOUSE CATS**.

CAT'S EYES

Big cats are large, long-legged, and higher off the ground than most small cats. Many big cats search for prey rather than ambush it. They rely more on muscle than visual accuracy to capture prey. As it happens, their vision is similar to ours: Big cats have **PUPILS THAT REMAIN ROUND** when they contract (get smaller). Most small cats (with the exception of the cheetah) often hunt in low light and ambush prey that comes close to them; they rely more on seeing prey and accurately pouncing on it than on subduing it with their strength. To help them do that, their **PUPILS CHANGE TO VERTICAL SLITS** when they contract. Round pupils aren't as efficient as vertical ones. They dilate (get bigger) and contract more slowly and offer less depth perception.

ROUND PUPILS

VERTICAL SLITS

ROAR VS. PURR

Generally speaking, **BIG CATS** roar—except for snow leopards, which make a chuffing sound instead—but they are not able to purr. Some can make a purr-like noise when they exhale, but researchers usually don't consider this to be a true purr. Here's why: All cats have a U-shape hyoid bone in their throats that helps to support the tongue and larynx (where the vocal cords are). In big cats, the hyoid is flexible and attached to the skull with a ligament; this makes purring impossible, but (except for in the case of the snow leopard) it allows them to roar. (A snow leopard has a flexible hyoid but not the right configuration of the larynx to roar.) Lions and tigers roar the loudest, and lions can sometimes be heard for more than 5 miles.

SMALL CATS can not roar, but they can purr both when breathing in and when breathing out. This is because their hyoid bone is firmly in place. When a small cat's larynx vibrates, the hyoid bone resonates, causing a purring sound.

BIG CAT COLLECTIONS

A group of jaguars is called a shadow; leopards, a leap; lions, a pride or sawt; tigers, a streak or ambush.

DID YOU KNOW?

A **TIGON** results from a cross between a female lion and a male tiger. Found only in captivity, tigons grow to be about 9 feet long and weigh between 200 and 500 pounds.

A **LIGER** is a cross between a female tiger and a male lion, rarely found in the wild and then only in India's Gir Forest. It can grow to be 11 feet long and weigh 900 pounds.

JAGUAR

LEOPARD

SPOT THE DIFFERENCES

Can't tell a jaguar from a leopard? Take a closer look (but not too close)! **JAGUARS** are bigger, stockier, and stronger than **LEOPARDS,** with shorter tails. A jaguar's rosettes are rose-shape black circles around a lighter color, with spots in the center. Leopards have smaller, plain rosettes.

BIG CAT MATCH GAME

1. Species of this big cat can be found in about 13 Asian countries in a variety of habitats, including evergreen and temperate forests, tropical rain forests, mangrove swamps, grasslands, and savannas. These cats prefer a solitary life and can run as fast as 40 miles per hour and leap more than 12 feet high.

2. These cats can be found in sub-Saharan Africa in deserts, grasslands, savannas, scrub, and open woodlands. There are also a few hundred in India's Gir Forest. These are the only big cats that live in groups. They can run at up to 50 mph for short periods but spend up to 20 hours each day resting or sleeping.

3. These solitary cats live in Africa and Asia in a variety of environments, including desert and arid regions, grasslands, savannas, mountains, and rain forests. Their long tail helps with balance as they easily climb trees, stashing their food within the branches, away from other predators. These cats can run for short periods at up to 37 mph.

4. Solitary by nature, these cats live in Central and South America, with rare sightings in the southwestern United States. Found in rain forests, deciduous forests, grasslands, savannas, swamps, scrub, and deserts, these cats have the most powerful bite of any big cat relative to their size. They can run for short periods at up to 31 mph.

5. These shy cats are well suited to surviving in the harsh, rugged, mountainous terrain of the 12 Central and South Asian countries in which they live. Their long tail helps them to balance when traveling across steep, rocky land and acts as a muffler in cold weather. Powerful hind legs enable these cats to leap vertically—as high as 19 feet!

SAVE THE CATS

All big cat populations are struggling due to hunting, habitat reduction, or other issues. Tigers are of the greatest concern. They are listed as endangered, which means that there is a very high risk of extinction in the wild in the immediate future: Only between 3,000 and 4,000 of these felines are believed to exist in the world. Lions, leopards, and snow leopards are listed as vulnerable, a grade below endangered, while jaguars are listed as near-threatened, a step below vulnerable. Check out your favorite wildlife rescue organization or sanctuary—they may offer several ways in which you can help to save the big cats.

__ **A.** Jaguar

__ **B.** Leopard

MATCH EACH BIG CAT
DESCRIPTION (OPPOSITE) WITH
ITS CORRESPONDING PHOTO.

__ **C.** Lion

__ **D.** Tiger

__ **E.** Snow Leopard

ANSWERS:
1. D; 2. C; 3. B; 4. A; 5. E

Craft Some Pinecone Critters!

When you walk through the woods, collect items that you find like leaves, flowers, and twigs to make crafts. If you find some pinecones, try making these cone critters!

YOU WILL NEED:
pinecones
acrylic paint
paintbrushes
pieces of felt
fabric scissors
glue gun*
small black pom-poms
flat-sided beads,
    color of your choice

*Ask for an adult's help when using a glue gun.

1. Paint the pinecones and allow them to dry completely.
2. Cut the pieces of felt into circles for faces and half-circles and/or triangles for ears.
3. Cut out a 90-degree triangle wedge from each felt circle.
4. Overlap the two cut edges and glue them together to make a cone.
5. Glue on a small pom-pom to make a nose and two beads to make eyes.
6. Put some glue on the inside of the felt cone and press onto one end of the pinecone.
7. Put a small amount of glue on the felt half-circles and stick them on the critter's head to make ears.

MAKE WAY FOR DUCK STAMPS

Do you like to collect stamps? Gathering Federal Duck Stamps can be a fun way to not only add to your collection but also help to protect wildlife habitat. These stamps, often required to hunt wildfowl, also allow people to enter national wildlife refuges without paying a fee. In addition, the stamps' stunning artwork has attracted the eyes of collectors.

STAMP RIGHT UP!

Want to see your artwork on a stamp? Give it a try by entering the Junior Duck Stamp Art Contest for young artists in grades K–12.

To enter, you'll need to . . .

- pick a native North American duck, swan, or goose from a list of eligible species
- research the behavior, habitat, and look of your bird of choice
- choose an eligible medium, such as paint, ink, or crayon
- include a conservation message along with your artwork (this part is optional)

"Best of Show" winners of the state, territory, and district contests compete at the national level. The art that wins the national contest will be displayed on a Junior Duck Stamp, which will be offered for sale to the public! *(continued)*

U.S. FISH AND WILDLIFE SERVICE
$5
NORTHERN PINTAIL
C. CLAYTON (OH)
2012-2013 JUNIOR DUCK STAMP

U.S. FISH AND WILDLIFE SERVICE
$5
WOOD DUCK
L. SPANG (OH)
2009-2010 JUNIOR DUCK STAMP

U.S. FISH AND WILDLIFE SERVICE
$5
RING-NECKED DUCKS
A. HUNTER (IL)
2011-2012 JUNIOR DUCK STAMP

U.S. FISH AND WILDLIFE SERVICE
$5
FULVOUS WHISTLING-DUCK
A. NISBETT (MO)
2004-2005 JUNIOR DUCK STAMP

U.S. FISH AND WILDLIFE SERVICE
$5
AMERICAN WIGEONS
P. WILLEY (AR)
15TH ANNIVERSARY
2007-2008 JUNIOR DUCK STAMP

U.S. FISH AND WILDLIFE SERVICE
$5
TRUMPETER SWAN
A. McCANN (MN)
2001-2002 JUNIOR DUCK STAMP

U.S. FISH AND WILDLIFE SERVICE
$5
MALLARDS
N. CLOSSON (MT)
2002-2003 JUNIOR DUCK STAMP

U.S. FISH AND WILDLIFE SERVICE
$5
RINGNECK
K. NELSON (WI)
2005-2006 JUNIOR DUCK STAMP

Junior duck stamps can be purchased for $5 each. The money supports environmental education programs and recognition of students' efforts. To learn more, go to fws.gov/birds and search for "junior duck stamp" to find the information page. Submissions are due at different times, depending on where you live. Make sure to read all of the rules and regulations, and—most important of all—be creative!

THE YOUNGEST WINNER

Madison Grimm of Burbank, South Dakota, was 6 years old when she won the Junior Duck Stamp Art Contest in 2013 with her oil painting of a canvasback duck.

STAMP STUNNERS

● Depending on condition and features, the first year's duck stamps, which originally cost $1, can be worth up to $10,500!

● The largest assemblage of Federal Duck Stamps is the Jeanette C. Rudy collection. Gathered over 50 years, it features the very first duck stamp ever sold (in 1934), along with misprints and other rarities. You can see these stamps at the Smithsonian National Postal Museum in Washington, D.C.

U.S. FISH AND WILDLIFE SERVICE
$5
TRUMPETER SWANS
ISAAC SCHREIBER (VA)
2017-2018 JUNIOR DUCK STAMP

U.S. FISH AND WILDLIFE SERVICE
$5
KING EIDER
SI YOUN KIM (NJ)
2014-2015 JUNIOR DUCK STAMP

U.S. FISH AND WILDLIFE SERVICE
$5
WOOD DUCKS
R. KIRBY (IL)
1999-2000 JUNIOR DUCK STAMP

U.S. FISH AND WILDLIFE SERVICE
$5
CANADA GOOSE
S. RUSSELL (CA)
1997-98 JUNIOR DUCK STAMP

HOW IT ALL BEGAN

In 1934, conservationists and naturalists became concerned about the increasing destruction of wetland habitat important to the survival of waterfowl. In response—and with the encouragement of Jay "Ding" Darling, a cartoonist, artist, and conservationist—President Franklin D. Roosevelt signed the Migratory Bird Hunting Stamp Act, also called the "Duck Stamp Act."

This act required waterfowl hunters who were 16 or older to purchase a stamp annually, and it created a fund for the proceeds from these sales. Ninety-eight cents of every dollar raised from the sale of duck stamps is used to purchase or lease waterfowl habitat in order to protect it.

Since 1949, the art for the adult duck stamp has been chosen through a national art contest in which participants create nature-inspired pieces of native waterfowl. The Junior Duck Stamp Art Contest was started in 1993 to get young artists involved. Some of the past winners are shown throughout this story.

DYNAMIC
DART
FROGS

Most animals try to blend in with their surroundings, but don't tell this to poison dart frogs!

CONSPICUOUS COLORS

POISON DART FROGS' bright colors stand out against the rain forest's many shades of green and brown, so predators have an easy time spotting the tiny frogs (they can be as small as your thumbnail!). The predators quickly learn, however, that munching on these bright colors results in a toxic taste! This is an example of aposematic coloration, which is a bold coloring or pattern that warns predators, "Don't eat me—I'm poisonous!"

YOU ARE WHAT YOU EAT

POISON DART FROGS are not naturally poisonous. They get their toxicity from their food. A typical poison dart frog diet consists of small invertebrates such as ants, beetles, and mites, some of which carry poisons. When the frogs eat these, their toxicity builds up in the frogs' skin. In fact, poison dart frogs that do not get their usual rain forest diet—like those kept in captivity—are not poisonous.

DID YOU KNOW?

Poison dart frogs aren't the only toxic animals to get their poison from food. Others include the hooded pitohui bird of New Guinea, keelback snakes of Southeast Asia, and MALAGASY POISON FROGS of Madagascar!

PIGGYBACKING POLLYWOGS

In the amphibian world, POISON DART FROGS are some of the best parents a tadpole could ask for. Once a poison dart frog's eggs hatch, the tadpoles wriggle up onto a parent's back. Then, like a tiny tadpole school bus, the frog delivers its offspring to small pools of water, where the tadpoles will live and develop for several weeks. Anything from a puddle to a hollowed-out stump makes a suitable home.

EGG-CELLENT PARENTS

Female STRAWBERRY POISON DART FROGS ensure that their babies survive by regularly feeding the tadpoles unfertilized eggs. Aside from being the tadpoles' main source of food, these eggs contain some of the same toxins that the parents have, giving the tadpoles a head start on building up their own toxicity.

DANGEROUS DARTS

Indigenous (local) peoples in South America traditionally used the toxic skin secretions from GOLDEN POISON DART FROGS to cover the tips of their hunting arrows and blow darts. The poison-tipped projectiles made hunting birds and other game a lot easier. Hunters needed to handle their weapons with care, though: One golden poison dart frog produces enough toxin to kill two fully grown elephants!

CREATE YOUR OWN COLORFUL FROGS

Transform these frogs into works of art! Ask an adult to make copies of these pages so that you can create a chorus* of frogs.

*A GROUP OF FROGS IS CALLED A
CHORUS, ARMY, OR COLONY.

Eyes on the Skies for Dragonflies!

With their big eyes and beautiful, jewel-like colors, dragonflies are one of the most recognizable insects in the world. These fascinating creatures are powerful hunters and exciting to watch in action.

The first dragonfly ancestors appeared on Earth 300 to 350 million years ago. Scientists have found fossils of huge dragonfly-like insects that had wingspans of more than 28 inches. One of the largest modern-day dragonflies in North America, the giant darner, has a wingspan of about 5 inches.

LIVIN' LIFE

Dragonflies have three life stages: egg, nymph, and adult. A female dragonfly lays a few hundred to more than a thousand eggs at a time in water, on or in aquatic plants, or in mudbanks.

Nymphs hatch out of the eggs and can not fly. They commonly live in aquatic environments like lakes, rivers, and streams; some live in water-filled tree cavities or in saltwater habitats, such as mangroves or salt marshes. Dragonfly nymphs have gills inside their abdomen that take in oxygen from the water.

As dragonfly nymphs grow, they must shed their exoskeletons (the outer part of their bodies) so that they can become larger. This is called "molting." Dragonfly nymphs will molt between 6 and 15 times, depending on the species.

"Emergence" is the process that occurs during the last molt, as a dragonfly nymph changes into an adult dragonfly. The nymph crawls out of the water and sits on a plant or rock so that it can adapt to breathing air. After a while, the skin of the nymph splits open and a dragonfly that looks like an adult breaks out. This happens fairly fast—in about 1 to 3 hours!

Newly emerged dragonflies have soft bodies. They can not fly, and they are not brightly colored. It takes only a few hours or days before they grow stronger and are able to fly. They remain this way typically for up to 2 weeks, until they become fully mature adults.

Dragonflies may live for about 6 months to a few years. Most of this time is spent in nymph form, with adults usually living for a few weeks or months. Some species, such as the dragonhunter, can live for up to 7 years, mainly as nymphs.

GET A BETTER LOOK

An adult dragonfly has two large eyes and three small eyes. The large eyes are compound, meaning that they are made up of many lenses. Because of the eyes' positions in the head, dragonflies can see in almost every direction at the same time.

Both adult and nymph dragonflies have three pairs of legs. If a nymph is caught by a predator, it can afford to lose a leg to free itself. The leg will be replaced when the insect molts again.

Adult dragonflies have two pairs of sheer wings. Their four wings move independently of one another, giving them the ability to fly forward, backward, and sideways—or to just hover in place. They are strong, fast fliers. Some species can fly at up to 30 miles per hour!

Feeding Time!

Dragonflies are carnivores. The nymphs eat other types of insect nymphs, such as those of caddisflies, mayflies, and stoneflies. They also like to munch on snails, mosquito larvae, and young fish. Adult dragonflies eat mosquitoes, deerflies, horseflies, midges, and many other kinds of insects.

Birds such as hawks, purple martins, and swifts like to eat adult dragonflies. Nymphs are food for fish, frogs, and turtles.

The Damsel and the Dragon

Damselflies look a lot like dragonflies. They are related, but there are many ways to tell them apart. One way is to watch them when they perch on something. Most damselflies fold their wings above and along their abdomen. When most dragonflies perch, their wings stay flat and out to the sides. Another difference is that damselflies have eyes that are widely separated, whereas dragonfly eyes are close together.

FAST FACTS!

- There are more than 3,000 species of dragonflies in the world. North America has about 330.

- The only place in the world where you won't find a dragonfly is Antarctica—it's too cold!

- One dragonfly may eat from 30 to hundreds of mosquitoes per day.
- Dragonflies beat their wings about 30 times per second.
- A group of dragonflies is known as a swarm.
- The hobby of dragonfly watching is called "oding," because the insects belong to the order Odonata and are called odonates.

Lore and More

- Dragonflies are a symbol of good luck in Chinese tradition.
- Many cultures believe that it is good luck if a dragonfly lands on you.
- Dragonflies have been a symbol of purity, activity, and swiftness for some Native Americans.
- Some common names for dragonflies are "mosquito hawk," "devil's darning needle," and "snake doctor."

DIY DRAGONFLY

Make a dragonfly from some simple supplies! Ask for an adult's help when using a glue gun.

YOU WILL NEED:
1 wooden clothespin
glitter paints or markers
glue gun
2 googly eyes
2 pipe cleaners

❶ Paint your dragonfly's body (clothespin) with as many colors as you want.
❷ Put a small drop of glue at the end of the clothespin near the metal bracket.
❸ Press two googly eyes onto the glue.
❹ To make a pair of wings, take one end of a pipe cleaner and bend it toward the center; twist the end around the center so that it stays in place. Repeat with the other end of the pipe cleaner.
❺ Using the other pipe cleaner, repeat step 4 to make another pair of wings.
❻ Put a small drop of glue in the center of one of the wing pairs and then press the other pair on top. Nudge the top pair a little so that its wing loops don't overlap those of the other pair.
❼ Open the clothespin and then put a small drop of glue into the groove that's on the inside of the clothespin.
❽ Press the center of the wings onto the glue and then close the clothespin on the wings.

LOOK WHAT I FOUND?!!

Every now and then, in the middle of what seems like an ordinary day, completely unexpected things can happen.

FROM TRASH TO TREASURE

Sometimes it pays to take a second look. Just ask 13-year-old Luca Malaschnitschenko. He and amateur archaeologist René Schön were using metal detectors to treasure hunt on the German island of Ruegen when Luca found a small piece of metal. He thought that it was simply a piece of trash, but then he cleaned it off and took a closer look.

Luca and René brought their discovery to the German archaeology office, where it was confirmed that they had found a piece of Viking silver. The pair was asked to keep quiet about their discovery until a team had time to return to the island and conduct a professional excavation for additional artifacts.

Several months later, Luca and his friend were invited to participate in the excavation. The dig area covered almost an acre, and the team uncovered treasure from the reign of a famous Danish Viking king, Harald Gormsson. They found around 600 silver objects, including coins, rings, pearls, necklaces, and a charm called a "Thor's hammer."

OLD NAME, NEW TECHNOLOGY

King Harald was nicknamed "Bluetooth," probably because he had a dead tooth that looked blue. Does this name sound familiar? The modern wireless technology was named after Harald, the Viking king. Several engineers who developed it had been reading about Vikings and decided to use the code name "Bluetooth" for their project. The name stuck.

UNDERWATER SURPRISE

"**D**ad, I found a sword!," 8-year-old Saga Vanecek shouted one summer day to her father. She had been crawling around in Sweden's Lake Vidostern, searching for stones to skip across the water. On this day, the lake water was especially low. Saga felt something strange buried in the clay and sand and pulled out a long, rusty object. When she noticed that it had a point at one end and a handle at the other, she lifted it into the air. "I felt like a warrior, but Daddy said I looked like Pippi Longstocking," she later wrote in a newspaper article about the experience. (Pippi Longstocking is a fictional 9-year-old girl with red pigtails whose adventures are described in a series of children's books.)

The sword looked old and fragile, and neighbors guessed that it might be a Viking sword. After Saga and her father showed the sword to an archaeologist, they were told that it was at least 1,000 years old. After further analysis, it was determined that the 33-inch sword, which also included a sheath (a cover) made of wood and leather, was actually about 1,500 years old—even older than the Vikings!

Several months later, an archaeological team returned to the lake to search for more objects. They found a brooch as old as the sword and a coin from the 18th century. Saga donated the sword to a local museum. Although she was disappointed to part with her find, she is happy that others will get to see it.

"Now, whenever I go swimming in the lake, I will be looking to see what I can find," she says. "It feels like that lake might be a little bit magic."

BONES IN THE BADLANDS

Twelve-year-old Nathan Hrushkin has wanted to be a paleontologist since he was 6. Every summer, he and his dad go on fossil-hunting outings. Their 2020 trip to Horseshoe Canyon in the badlands of Alberta, Canada, was unforgettable! (Badlands are usually a barren region with harsh terrain.)

Nathan went to check out an area where they had previously found bone fragments. He spotted something and shouted for his father. Hearing the urgency in his son's voice, Dion Hrushkin hurried to his side.

"When I looked at it, it was very, very obviously a bone," Nathan says. "It looked like a bone that you'd see in a TV show." They noted their GPS position and sent photos of Nathan's find to the Royal Tyrrell Museum of Paleontology in Drumheller, Alberta. Scientists there reported that the fossil was the humerus bone of a young hadrosaur—a duck-billed dinosaur that lived about 69 million years ago.

"I was basically just breathless," Nathan recalls. "I was so excited that I didn't feel that excited, I was just so in shock."

Hadrosaur fossils are a common find in the area, but few juvenile fossils had been discovered. Soon museum crews arrived on the site and uncovered between 30 and 50 additional hadrosaur bones. Nathan and his father were invited back to the site to watch them work.

"This young hadrosaur is a very important discovery because it comes from a time interval for which we know very little about what kind of dinosaurs or animals lived in Alberta," reports curator François Therrien. "Nathan and Dion's find will help us to fill this big gap in our knowledge of dinosaur evolution."

Nathan is already looking forward to his next adventure. "Every year we've come here, we've found something a little bit better than the past year," he says. "Now we have to try to outdo ourselves."

BACKYARD DETECTIVE

Y ou are never too young to help to make an important discovery. When Sylvie Beckers was 2 years old, she discovered a new species of treehopper (a plant-eating insect). Of course, it helped that her mother, Laura Sullivan-Beckers, was a biology professor at Murray State University in Kentucky.

Sylvie and her mom were planting wildflowers when the girl accidentally overwatered the flower bed. Hundreds of dead treehoppers began to float in the puddle. Sylvie's mom recognized many, but not the ones shaped like bright green raindrops.

Over the summer, Sylvie helped her mom to collect more than 1,000 treehoppers, including about 70 of the unfamiliar species. Sylvie's mom sent the specimens to an expert to help to determine whether this treehopper was a new species or a type normally seen in South or Central America that might have migrated north. After much research, the scientists announced that this was indeed a new type of treehopper, and they named it after Sylvie: *Hebetica sylviae.*

Her mother notes: "I was at the right place at the right time with the perfect field assistant." Sylvie, by then 5, called herself a "half-scientist."

WARRIORS

charge to protect our planet!

RIVER GUARDIAN

Stella Bowles wanted to swim in the LaHave River in front of her Nova Scotia home, but her mother said no. She explained to Stella that many of the nearby houses had "straight pipes" that emptied toilet waste directly into the river even though such pipes are illegal. Stella nicknamed the waterway "Poo River" and decided to focus her sixth-grade science fair project on the problem.

While doing research, Stella learned that 600 straight pipes emptied into the LaHave River! She tested the water for human waste and made her results public. The project earned her international recognition. She convinced the Canadian government to pledge $15.7 million to help clean up the river and replace all of the pipes with more environmentally friendly systems.

Stella was named an International Young Eco-Hero, cowrote a book called *My River: Cleaning Up the LaHave River,* and now leads workshops to teach other kids how to test water for contamination. "My hope is that I can inspire more people—of any age—to take on a cause they believe in and make change," she says. "Every little act of kindness to our Earth helps."

PRAIRIE PROTECTOR

When Trevor Burke first visited the Blackland Prairie at age 11, he loved the unique Texas landscape—a 300-mile-long ecosystem running from the Red River in North Texas southward to San Antonio. The Dallas native marveled at its black, spongy soil, and its tall grasses reminded him of cotton candy. But Trevor discovered that this prairie was one of the most ecologically threatened regions in the world. Only 5,000 of its original 12 million acres remained, due in part to agricultural development, grazing, mining, and urbanization.

After consulting with Texas master naturalists and other experts, Trevor organized a team of volunteers. Together they removed invasive grass species and planted native alternatives. The next step was to reintroduce endangered Texas wildlife, including the northern bobwhite quail, whose population had declined by 82 percent in the previous 50 years.

Trevor learned about incubating eggs—by doing it in his own living room! He raised over 300 quail, eventually moving them to a special area in his backyard. "They learn to walk, learn to poop, and chirp constantly," he notes. When the birds were big enough, Trevor helped tag and release them into the Blackland Prairie.

Trevor won many awards, including a college scholarship, for his environmental activism. He encourages others to get involved: "Each of us has the capability, power, passion, and responsibility to preserve and protect our world." *(continued)*

CHANGE MAKER

Audrey Lin does more than just help the planet when she recycles. This crafty native of Watertown, Massachusetts, has a passion for transforming things, such as when she spins her own fiber and dyes it, using black beans and walnuts. As part of a 6-week summer student leadership program, which took her to India, she learned how to transform plastic shopping bags into lightweight, waterproof sleeping mats. When she returned to her school, Audrey started a program called Matting Change and taught others how to create the mats.

Audrey says that each mat requires between 600 and 700 plastic shopping bags, plus 15 to 20 hours of labor. The first step is making plastic yarn, which she calls "plarn," from the bags. She then crochets the plarn into a sleeping mat. Audrey donates the finished mats to a nearby homeless shelter. The plarn doesn't attract bedbugs or lice, so the sleeping mats are clean and safe to use.

Audrey is also a climate activist, working with a youth advocacy group called the Sunrise Movement, whose goal is to stop climate change. She urges her peers to "look beyond just yourself and your world—try to see a bigger picture."

CLEANUP CRAFTER

You're never too young to help the environment. Just ask Ryan Moralevitz of Florida, who at age 6 was a winner in the Youth Ocean Conservation Film Competition with his entry "The Pollution Solution." He and his family often picked up trash while walking along the oceanfront. After he watched some older kids dump a tire into the ocean, he was inspired to learn about pollution's effects on sea life.

Soon thereafter, he started his "The Fishes Wishes" project, which involved making magnets and ornaments out of driftwood, selling them at fairs and shops, and donating the proceeds to the Ocean Conservancy. He wrote a book called *Puffy the Pufferfish Saves the Ocean* and now also sells key chains and suncatchers made from recycled wood, stones, and natural materials. Ryan had donated over $10,000 to ocean conservation groups as of 2019. *(continued)*

ADVENTUROUS RECYCLER

"Anyone can make a difference—you just have to start somewhere," says Joslyn Stamp, a busy sixth grader from Plattsmouth, Nebraska. Joslyn is always looking for ways to help to protect and educate people about the environment. She won a President's Environmental Youth Award for an ongoing project that she started in fourth grade to collect permanent markers, highlighters, and dry erase markers that would otherwise end up in landfills. She has already gathered over 10,000 markers!

At least once a month, Joslyn collects old markers from a library, 4-H office, daycare, local moms group, and several schools. The writing implements are counted and packaged by Joslyn and her younger sister Maggie before being shipped to Crayola to be repurposed as part of their ColorCycle program. (Find out how to recycle your own school's used markers at Crayola.com/colorcycle.aspx.)

Joslyn also acts as a Buddy Bison Student Ambassador with the National Park Trust, traveling to a national park once each month and writing about her experiences on social media. The avid hiker and adventurer shares tips to help others appreciate and protect these special places. "I can tell kids about how amazing the national parks are and all of the amazing things that you can do there," she says.

WANT TO HELP?

Explore award-winning projects and learn how to get involved at Epa.gov/education/presidents-environmental-youth-award.

THE LIGHTS-OUT KIDS

When Colorado governor Jared Polis announced a series of environmental initiatives for his state, a group of fourth- and fifth-grade students called the Green Team Superheroes, from Wilmot Elementary in Evergreen, stood by his side wearing their signature green capes. The team had previously won a President's Environmental Youth Award for making their school more energy-efficient.

Each Green Team member was assigned a classroom to monitor. Using light meters, they determined that most classrooms were overlit. Plus, many devices were plugged in but not being used, thus consuming a small amount of power called "phantom energy."

The team suggested ways to reduce energy costs—such as removing almost two-thirds of unnecessary classroom lightbulbs and unplugging devices. (Learn how to monitor energy usage at your school at Nwf.org/eco-schools-USA.)

In one school year, the Green Team Superheroes saved the school more than $1,300 and achieved the highest Eco-Schools USA award, the Green Flag, from the National Wildlife Federation's green school program. "They have come together as a team," observes parent volunteer and program founder Lisa Dewil. "They have taken this idea and made it their own." As the Superheroes themselves like to say, "Together we made a difference!"

CRACKING THE

Coconuts can be found in everything from our food and water to beauty products and household objects. They have even been used to make gas masks—but we'll get into that later. First, let's explore the coconut's origins and how it got its name.

WHERE DID IT COME FROM?

Coconuts are common throughout the tropics, but they are not all the same even though they all come from just one species. Over time, as the plants grew in the wild in different places or were bred by humans, they developed different traits, such as having round or egg-shape fruit. The coconut is the fruit of the coconut palm tree, and, technically, it is a drupe, not a nut. A drupe is a fruit that has an outer layer covering a fibrous, tough, or fleshy part that in turn surrounds a hard shell that contains a seed. (The coconuts that you see in grocery stores have had their outer and middle fibrous layers removed.)

"Coco" comes from the Portuguese and Spanish words for "grinning face," because 16th-century Portuguese sailors thought that the three indentations on the shell resembled a grinning monkey or goblin. "Nut" was added later by English-speakers, presumably because they thought that it resembled a large nut.

COCONUT

COOL COCONUT CONCOCTIONS

- During World Wars I and II, gas masks made with activated carbon from burned coconut shells were common. After the shells are burned and specially processed, the resulting charcoal has many small holes that trap toxins and chemicals.
- Coir is made from coarse fibers taken from the middle layer of a coconut. It can be found in a variety of products, including doormats, brooms, ropes, mattress stuffing, and gardening medium.
- Coconut oil is used a lot in home remedies. You can use it in your hair to condition split ends, swish it in your mouth for several minutes to improve the health of your teeth and gums (called "oil pulling"), and apply it to your body as a moisturizer to soften dry skin.

COOKING WITH COCONUTS

Coconuts have many uses, but their most familiar place is in the kitchen. Whether you like coconut milk, water, oil, flour, or the white meat of the coconut (called "copra" when dried), it's good to know that coconuts are full of vitamins and minerals. Try these recipes, and soon you'll be crazy for coconuts!

COCONUT BANANA SMOOTHIE

You Will Need:
blender
cup
paper or metal straw

1 frozen banana
½ cup coconut milk
2 tablespoons maple syrup
1 tablespoon wheat germ
1 teaspoon vanilla extract

1. Add all of the ingredients to the blender and process until smooth.

2. Pour into a cup and add a straw.

Makes 1 smoothie.

COCONUT OATMEAL COOKIES

You Will Need:

2 baking sheets
parchment paper
mixing bowl
wooden spoon
oven mitt or pot holder
spatula
wire cooling rack
½ cup (1 stick) butter, softened
½ cup sugar

½ cup brown sugar
1 egg
1 teaspoon vanilla extract
1 cup all-purpose flour
½ teaspoon baking powder
½ teaspoon baking soda
¼ teaspoon salt
1 cup quick-cooking oats
½ cup unsweetened shredded coconut

Convert to metric on p. 186

1. Preheat oven to 350°F.

2. Line the baking sheets with parchment paper.

3. In the bowl, combine butter, sugar, and brown sugar. Stir well until smooth.

4. Add the egg and vanilla and stir again until creamy.

5. Add the flour, baking powder, baking soda, and salt. Stir until smooth.

6. Add the oats and coconut and stir until incorporated.

7. Take a small amount of dough, about the size of a golf ball, roll it between your hands, and place on the baking sheet. Repeat with the remaining dough.

8. Bake for 9 to 12 minutes, or until golden.

9. Use the spatula to move cookies to wire racks to cool completely.

Makes about 36 cookies.

AUSTRALIA: toast with Vegemite (a thick, brown, salty food paste)

BRAZIL: cheese puffs

BREAKFAST
Around the
WORLD

What is your favorite breakfast food? Maybe in the morning you like to eat cereal or bacon and eggs or blueberry muffins. While those are typical foods to eat in the United States and Canada, kids in other countries crave different morning meals. Here's how some of them start the day.

CHINA: rice porridge, often topped with pickled vegetables, eggs, or meat

EGYPT:
stewed beans
topped with
chopped
hard-boiled
eggs

INDIA: porridge-like dish made
from dry-roasted
semolina or coarse rice flour

ISRAEL:
eggs poached in seasoned
tomato sauce

JAMAICA:
fruit and
salted fish

MEXICO: tortilla chips in red or green sauce

MOROCCO: fava bean soup topped with olive oil

MYANMAR: catfish noodle soup

NETHERLANDS: toast topped with chocolate, vanilla, or fruit-flavor candy sprinkles

PERU:
plantain fritters with pork

RUSSIA: porridge cooked
with milk and sugar

PORTUGAL: egg custard tarts

VENEZUELA: cheese-filled corn pancakes

Fun and Flavorful!

**Have you ever heard the expression "you eat with your eyes"?
This means that when food is visually pleasing,
or looks good, you will want to eat it. Dig into these easy
recipes that will satisfy your hungry eyes.**

BANANA SUSHI

You Will Need:
knife
plate
bananas
peanut butter, almond butter,
   or sunflower butter
honey
hazelnut chocolate spread
variety of toppings such as shredded
   coconut, mini marshmallows,
   chocolate shavings, crushed cereal,
   cinnamon and sugar, rainbow
   sprinkles

1. Cut each banana into three pieces.

2. Dip a banana piece into one of the sticky ingredients (peanut butter, honey, hazelnut chocolate spread).

3. Roll each banana piece in one of the toppings.

4. Place finished banana on the plate and continue with remaining bananas, mixing and matching different toppings.

Convert to metric on p. 186

BAKED POTATO MICE

You Will Need:

fork
baking sheet
knife
spoon
bowl
toothpicks
russet potatoes
butter
carrots
peas

1. Preheat the oven to 400°F.

2. Using the fork, prick holes all over the potatoes.

3. Place potatoes on the baking sheet and bake for 45 to 60 minutes.

4. Once potatoes are cool enough to touch, slice each one down the center.

5. Open a potato and spoon out some of the cooked potato into the bowl. Mash with a small amount of butter and then pile back into the potato.

6. Slice the carrots into thin rounds. (You can eat the pieces of carrot that you don't use to make the mouse.)

7. Place carrot rounds into the potato to make ears.

8. Place peas onto the mouse to make eyes and nose.

9. Insert toothpicks to make whiskers.

TROPICAL FRUIT TREES

You Will Need:

knife
plate
banana
kiwifruit
clementine or tangerine
frozen cranberries or
    blueberries, thawed

1. Peel a banana and cut in half lengthwise. Lay the halves, flat side down, on the plate.

2. Peel and cut the kiwifruit into long pieces. Place fruit at the top of each banana piece to look like palm leaves.

3. Peel and divide clementine into segments. Arrange beneath each banana tree and top with berries.

PIZZA FACES

You Will Need:

baking sheet
parchment paper
round pita bread
pizza sauce
shredded mozzarella cheese
**vegetables such as broccoli, cherry
    tomatoes, sliced zucchini, and peppers**

1. Preheat the oven to 350°F. Line the baking sheet with parchment paper.

2. Place pita on prepared baking sheet and spread with pizza sauce.

3. Sprinkle cheese over pita and add vegetables to build a face.

4. Bake for 5 minutes, or until cheese is melted.

OWL S'MORES

You Will Need:

**microwave-safe
    plate**
**graham crackers,
    broken in half**
marshmallows
yellow candy melts
chocolate chips
candy corn

1. Place graham cracker halves on the microwave-safe plate.

2. Cut marshmallows in half and place two halves side by side on each graham cracker half.

3. Top each marshmallow half with a candy melt.

4. Microwave the plated food for only 5 seconds.

5. Remove from the microwave and place a chocolate chip on each candy melt.

6. Place a piece of candy corn in the middle of the graham cracker just slightly touching the marshmallow eyes.

GAMES OF GLORY:
All About the Olympics

The ancient Greek Olympic Games took place every 4 years from 776 B.C. to at least A.D. 393. Most athletes were male soldiers; women could neither compete nor attend (probably because at that time, athletes competed naked). Chariot racing was always popular, as was wrestling, which (among other things) required men to carry live bulls around the stadium on their shoulders as a feat of strength.

After centuries with no Olympics, the Games were reborn in 1896. These first modern Olympic Games took place in Athens, Greece, as a nod to their historic origins. Athletes from 14 countries competed, with the largest teams representing Greece, Germany, France, and Great Britain. Currently, there are Summer and Winter Olympics; the winter events were first held in 1924.

Chloe Kim, 2018 Olympic gold medalist in women's snowboard halfpipe

SPORTS

YOUNG OLYMPIANS

You're never too young to follow your dreams.
With lots of hard work and practice, you can set records just like
these inspiring Olympians!

DIMITRIOS LOUNDRAS, AGE 10

A member of the Greek gymnastics team, Dimitrios competed in the 1896 Games. At 10 years and 218 days old, he became (and remains) the youngest Olympic athlete. Dimitrios's team placed third in the parallel bars, earning each member a bronze medal.

INGE SØRENSEN, AGE 12

In Berlin, Germany, Inge became the youngest female medalist in Olympic history when she won a bronze medal in the 200-meter breaststroke competition in 1936.

CHLOE KIM, AGE 17

At the 2018 Winter Games, Chloe Kim became the youngest woman to win an Olympic snowboarding gold medal when she won gold in the women's snowboard halfpipe.

TARA LIPINSKI, AGE 15

Tara became the youngest individual gold medalist when she won the Ladies' Singles ice-skating event at the 1998 Winter Games in Nagano, Japan. She was the youngest person to hold the titles of U.S., world, and Olympic champion.

THE MYSTERIOUS DUTCH ROWER

There may have been an Olympic competitor younger than Dimitrios Loundras. At the 1900 Olympics, a Dutch rowing team replaced one of their rowers with a young boy at the last minute. A photo shows him with rowers Françoise Brandt and Roelof Klein. His age and name are unknown. "This is the great mystery of Olympic history," says David Wallechinsky, an Olympic historian.

The 1900 World Olympics were a haphazard affair, lasting 5 months. Many athletes didn't even realize that they were competing in something called the "Olympic Games"!

NUMBER 1!

James Connolly won a scholarship to study at Harvard University in 1895, but a year later, he asked for a leave of absence to compete in the first modern Olympic Games. When authories refused his request, the 27-year-old withdrew and headed to Athens. He competed in and won the very first event of the Games—the triple jump, which was then called the "hop, skip, and jump." He became the first modern Olympic champion! James also went on to tie for second in the high jump and place third in the long jump.

FRIENDS FIRST

Two Japanese students reached the finals in the men's pole vault at the 1936 Olympics in Berlin. American Earle Meadows had earned the gold medal, leaving Shuhei Nishida and Sueo Oe to compete for silver and bronze. Since they were good friends, they wanted to stop competing and share the awards. However, officials would not allow this. Shuhei took the silver; Sueo, the bronze. (Shuhei vaulted 4 meters 25 centimeters in one try; Sueo took two tries.)

After the athletes returned to Japan, they had their medals cut in half and fused together. Their unique medals were called "The Medals of Friendship."

WELCOMING THE WOMEN

Women weren't allowed to compete in the Olympics until the 1900 Paris Games, when they entered lawn tennis and golf events. In 1912, in Stockholm, Sweden, women competed in swimming and diving for the first time. By 1928, in Amsterdam, Netherlands, women were finally being welcomed in track and field. However, after a few female athletes appeared to be exhausted after the 800-meter races, women's events longer than 200 meters were banned until 1960.

In Sarajevo, Yugoslavia, in 1984, skier Marja-Liisa Kirvesniemi-Hämäläinen of Finland became the only woman to compete in six different Olympics (earning three golds and a bronze).

Not until the 2012 London Olympics did female athletes from every competing country participate.

ABOUT THE MEDALS

Olympic gold medals are made mostly of silver. They're required to have about 6 grams of gold, according to Olympic rules. The last awards made entirely from gold were handed out at the 1912 Olympics in Stockholm, Sweden. The custom of awarding gold, silver, and bronze medals started in 1904 at the St. Louis Olympics.

A NEW ERA

English doctor Ludwig Guttmann founded the International Wheelchair Games in 1948 to help wounded veterans recover from World War II. These wheelchair competitions eventually became the Paralympic Games.

FROM PLAYGROUND TO PERFECTION

Nadia Comaneci began gymnastics lessons at age 6 in Romania after a coach spotted her turning cartwheels on the playground at recess. By age 14, she was dazzling the world at the 1976 Olympics in Montreal, Quebec, becoming the first gymnast in Olympic history to be awarded the perfect score of 10.0. The scoreboard hadn't been programmed to show such a high score! Instead, for her performance on the uneven bars, it said simply "1.00".

ALL-AROUND AWESOME

Simone Biles is the most decorated female Olympic gymnast of all time, with 25 medals to date—and 15 of these are gold! Not only is her name associated with Olympic greatness, but also she has four signature moves named after her. (Gymnasts can petition to have a unique move named after them after successfully landing it at a major competition.)

BELIEVE IT OR NOT!

When the Jamaican four-man bobsled team began training for the 1988 Winter Olympics in Calgary, Alberta, not a single member had ever been on a bobsled!

The team trained in a variety of places, including Austria and Lake Placid, New York, using borrowed equipment. In Calgary, during the third run of their competition, the driver lost control of the sled. After crashing at 85 mph, the team was disqualified—but not defeated. They got out of their bobsled and walked to the finish line as the crowd cheered. The courageous underdog story of the Jamaican bobsled team inspired the 1993 movie *Cool Runnings*.

WINNING ISN'T EVERYTHING

During Seoul, South Korea's 1988 Olympic Games, Canadian sailor Lawrence Lemieux was in second place in his race when he noticed that another competitor had overturned in danger-ous winds. He stopped to make a daring rescue of two injured sailors—and in the process disqualified himself from winning the race.

After the rescue, he still completed the course, beating 11 other competi-tors and finishing 21st out of 32 sailors.

For his heroism, Lawrence was awarded the Pierre de Coubertin medal for sportsmanship, one of the noblest honors given to an Olympic athlete.

OUT OF THIS WORLD

As a lead-up to the 2014 Olympics in Sochi, Russia, cosmonauts Oleg Kotov and Sergey Ryazanskiy carried the (unlit) Olympic Torch on a spacewalk. In addition, all of the astronauts aboard the International Space Station carried the torch relay-style throughout the spacecraft. As a result of this space venture, the Sochi Olympic Torch traveled farther than any other torch in history.

PENGUIN PUCKS

Starting with a numbered arrow, draw a path in the direction that the arrow takes you until you connect with the base of another arrow. Keep connecting arrows until you score a goal. Only one of the numbers will lead you on the right path, so choose carefully!

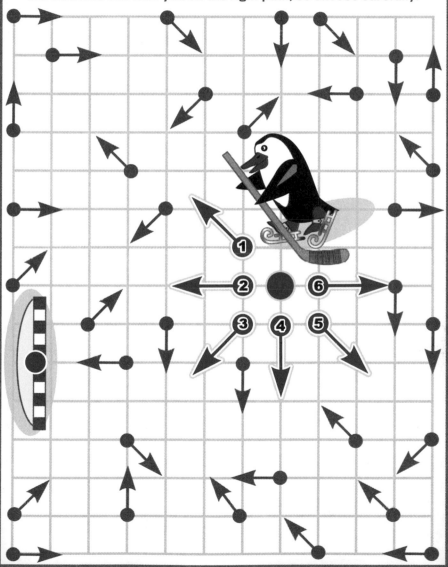

(SOLUTION ON PAGE 187.)

PEOPLE COULDN'T START THEIR **FROZEN CARS** TO GO TO THE GAME—
OR TO GET HOME AFTERWARD IF THEY MADE IT TO THE GAME
IN THE FIRST PLACE. **BUNDLE UP FOR . . .**

FROZEN FOOTBALL

THE PLAYING FIELD WAS A **SHEET OF ICE**
WITH A **ROCK-HARD SURFACE** LIKE **JAGGED CONCRETE.**

THE **ICEBOWL**

THE PLAYERS GOT **FROSTBITE** ON THEIR FINGERS AND TOES.

THE MARCHING BAND'S **INSTRUMENTS FROZE.**

THE FANS IN THE STANDS **ZIPPED THEMSELVES UP IN SLEEPING BAGS.**

THE OFFICIALS' METAL **WHISTLES FROZE** TO THEIR LIPS AND RIPPED THEM.

ONE SPECTATOR'S **EYELIDS FROZE SHUT.**

EVEN HOT BEVERAGES **FROZE SOLID.** ONE ANNOUNCER SAID. . .

I JUST TOOK A BITE OUT OF MY COFFEE!

WOULD YOU WANT TO PLAY IN—OR EVEN **GO TO**—A FOOTBALL GAME WITH CONDITIONS LIKE THESE?

ON DECEMBER 31, 1967, THAT'S EXACTLY WHAT PEOPLE DID WHEN THE GREEN BAY PACKERS AND THE DALLAS COWBOYS—PLUS 50,861 FANS IN THE STANDS—

COLD DRINKS HERE!

Convert to metric on p. 186

WITHSTOOD 3½ HOURS OF BRUTAL COLD AT WHAT WAS OFFICIALLY THE NATIONAL FOOTBALL LEAGUE'S CHAMPIONSHIP GAME BUT INSTEAD WILL BE FOREVER KNOWN AS THE **"ICE BOWL."** WHEN THE GAME STARTED, IT WAS −13°F:

THAT'S 13 DEGREES BELOW ZERO! THE WINDCHILL (WHAT IT FELT LIKE WHEN YOU ADDED THE WIND) WAS −36°F!

WHY DID THEY PLAY WHEN IT WAS THAT COLD?

FOOTBALL HAS TRADITIONALLY BEEN PLAYED IN EVERY KIND OF WEATHER.

RAIN	WIND	SNOW	COLD

BUT IT WAS **REALLY COLD**. WHY DIDN'T THEY POSTPONE THE GAME?

FOR ONE THING, MANY PREPARATIONS HAD ALREADY BEEN MADE, SUCH AS—

TV

RADIO

PLANE TICKETS

HOTEL ROOMS

BOTH TEAMS' FANS WERE ALREADY IN TOWN AND READY TO GO!

BACK IN 1967, FORECASTERS DIDN'T HAVE THE WEATHER RADAR AND SATELLITES THEY HAVE TODAY— NOR DID THEY

HAVE THE PREDICTION ACCURACY. WHEN A SUPER-FRIGID ARCTIC WEATHER FRONT SWEPT DOWN FROM CANADA

ON THE NIGHT BEFORE THE GAME, THE TEMPERATURE DROPPED ALMOST 30 DEGREES, SURPRISING A LOT OF PEOPLE!

THE LEAGUE THOUGHT THAT IT HAD A SPECIAL WEAPON TO FIGHT ANY EXTREME COLD: A NEWLY INSTALLED $80,000 UNDERGROUND HEATING SYSTEM THAT WOULD KEEP THE FIELD THAWED NO MATTER HOW COLD IT WAS.

THEY PUT A GIANT COVERING OVER THE FIELD ON THE NIGHT BEFORE TO KEEP THE HEAT IN, BUT THEY NEVER REALIZED THAT THIS WOULD TRAP ANY MOISTURE EVAPORATING FROM THE HEATED GROUND.

WHEN THEY TOOK THE COVER OFF ON GAME DAY, THE MOISTURE FELL BACK ONTO THE FIELD AND ALMOST INSTANTLY FROZE SOLID.

THE SHOW MUST GO ON! SO THEY PLAYED. PLAYERS, COACHES, AND OFFICIALS FOUND IT HARD TO MOVE.

THE PLAYERS COULD BARELY RUN AND INSTEAD HAD TO WOBBLE FLAT-FOOTED JUST TO STAY ON THEIR FEET.

THE FOOTBALL WAS AS HARD AS A ROCK.

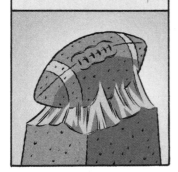

ON THE SIDELINES, PLAYERS WARMED THEIR FEET IN FRONT OF HEATERS UNTIL THE BOTTOMS OF THEIR SHOES MELTED.

THE TWO TEAMS COURAGEOUSLY BATTLED BACK AND FORTH UNTIL GREEN BAY SCORED THE WINNING POINTS WITH JUST 13 SECONDS LEFT IN THE GAME!

THE ORIGINAL 1967 ICE BOWL

EASTERN DALLAS 17
PACKERS 21

MINUTES
SECONDS 00

DOWN
TO GO

WESTERN

THE PACKERS AND COWBOYS WOULD GO DOWN IN HISTORY AS THE TRUE WINTER WARRIORS WHO HAD PLAYED IN WHAT TO THIS DAY IS STILL THE NFL'S COLDEST GAME.

The Pine Tar Incident

WOULD YOU BELIEVE THAT PINE TAR—YES, THAT STICKY STUFF ON PINE TREES—HAS EARNED A PLACE IN MAJOR LEAGUE BASEBALL'S SACRED RULE MANUAL? HERE IT IS:

Rule 3.02(c): If pine tar extends past the 18-inch limitation, then the umpire, on his own initiative or if alerted by the opposing team, shall order the batter to use a different bat. The batter may use the bat later in the game only if the excess substance is removed.

Huh? Well, let's start by explaining that pine tar is a sticky, tacky, oozy substance used by batters to get a stronger grip on the bat. The better the grip, the better the swing. The problem is, if the pine tar goes any higher than 18 inches on the bat, it can rub off on the ball when the batter hits it. . . . Usually, the rule doesn't cause

Convert to metric on p. 186

any problems, but one moment when it did kick up some dust involved one of the greatest hitters of all time, Kansas City Royals legend George Brett.

On July 24, 1983, the Royals were playing in New York against the Yankees. The visitors were behind by a score of 4–3. There was one Royal on base, with two outs, in the top of the ninth inning. When George Brett headed to home plate to hit, he wanted to send the ball soaring out of the park. And that's just what he did. He hit a two-run homer off the Yankees' ace relief pitcher, Goose Gossage, which put the Royals up 5–4. But the manager of the Yanks, Billy Martin, said, "Wait a minute, Georgie boy!" He thought that George's

bat had more pine tar on it than allowed, so he told the umpires.

*A*fter inspecting George's bat, the umpires decided that it was indeed in violation of the pine tar rule. They took back the homer and the two runs and called George out, which essentially gave the Yankees the win, seeing as how it was the top of the ninth and the Yanks were

ahead 4–3. When George heard the bad news, he charged at the umpires like a raging bull. He yelled, he hollered, he kicked up dust, and his eyes were stoked with fire. He was eventually ejected from the game, and the contest came to an end. The Yankees were victorious.

*T*he Royals fought the call against George, and after some detective work, the American League (AL) ruled that the amount of pine tar was not excessive. The AL ordered that the game be replayed from the point when George was at bat. And on August 18 of that year, the Royals officially won. The final score was 5–4.

Q:
WHY CAN'T YOUR NOSE
BE 12 INCHES LONG?

A:
BECAUSE THEN IT
WOULD BE A FOOT.

KNOW Your NOSE

your nose does so much more than smell things. It warms, moistens, and filters incoming air. When you take a breath through your nose, the air enters your nostrils, the two openings at the bottom of your nose. Then it travels up your nasal passages, one for each nostril. The passages are separated by your septum, a wall of cartilage near the entrance to your nose that becomes thin bone farther back. Next, the air enters a large opening called the nasal cavity. Finally, it travels down the back of the throat toward the lungs.

At the top of your nasal cavity, there is a small patch of nerve cells whose job is to detect odors. This area contains millions of these cells, called scent receptors. There are different types of scent receptors, each able to identify different shapes of odor molecules. When a breath carries a familiar molecule into this area, a receptor recognizes it and tells the brain.

THAT FLESHY BUTTON ON YOUR FACE
IS NOT THERE JUST TO TAKE UP SPACE.

YOUR NOSE CONTROLS YOUR SENSE OF SMELL
AND STUFFS UP WHEN YOU DON'T FEEL WELL.

BREATHE DEEP AND LET THE ODORS THROUGH,
THE FLOWERS, FOOD, AND, YES, DOG POO.

THE WORLD IS RICH WITH SCENTS GALORE,
SO USE YOUR NOSE—THAT'S WHAT IT'S FOR!

Anosmia (a-NAHZ-me-uh): complete loss of sense of smell

All "STUbbed" Up

Have you ever noticed that when you have a cold, it's harder to smell? When you're sick, your nasal passages swell and produce extra mucus that's thicker than usual. All this mucus is produced to trap whatever is invading your body, but it also blocks your nose and prevents odor molecules from reaching your scent receptors.

You might think that losing the ability to smell wouldn't be a big deal, but it can lead to a loss of taste and get you into dangerous situations, such as not being able to smell a gas leak or smoke from a fire. Up to 20 percent of people have difficulty in smelling.

Hyposmia (high-PAHZ-me-uh): lowered ability to smell

We're Lucky It's Yucky

The passages inside your nose are covered with a layer of mucus, that sticky liquid that you probably call "snot." Your body makes at least 4 cups of it every day. Mucus helps to keep you healthy!

NOSE-y News

Your nose protects you from danger. Bad smells often indicate that something should be avoided. A skunk uses its stinky spray to keep you away. Sour milk reeks so much that you would never drink it.

But what smells bad to you might smell delightful to another creature.

That Smell Is Swell!

- A scavenger like a turkey vulture is attracted to the smell of a dead animal.
- A dung beetle knows that the smell of poop means a delicious dinner.
- The corpse flower is a giant plant from Sumatra that, when in bloom, smells like a rotting body. When insects visit the plant to check out this inviting stench, they pollinate its flower.

How STINK Makes You THINK

Smells can make you feel good or bad depending on the memories that you associate with them. The aroma of sunscreen might make you happy as you recall beach vacations. The smell of antiseptic might make you anxious as you remember being a patient at the hospital. But your opinion of a smell can change, depending on new experiences. For example, have you ever become sick after eating something you liked? Afterward, your opinion of that food's smell likely changed from delicious to stomach-churning.

Q: WHAT DO YOU CALL A PERSON WITH NO BODY AND NO NOSE?

A: NOBODY NOSE.

Top JOBS for Top SNIFFERS

Got a powerful nose? These professions require a keen sense of smell (and sometimes lots of practice):

DEPARTMENT STORE PERFUME MANAGER: In charge of matching customers to their ideal scent.

AROMATHERAPIST: Works with scented oils to help alleviate client problems such as anxiety and stress.

AROMACHOLOGIST: Studies why and how scents trigger emotional responses.

ODOR TESTER: Able to precisely identify scents.

FRAGRANCE CHEMIST: Conducts research to develop and improve appealing scents.

Q: WHY IS YOUR NOSE IN THE MIDDLE OF YOUR FACE?

A: BECAUSE IT'S THE SCENTER.

N😊SING Around

• People once believed that humans could smell only about 10,000 different odors. Scientists recently upgraded that number to over 1 trillion.

• By focusing on what you smell, you may find that you are able to identify new scents, as well as get better at telling similar odors apart.

• You can notice some scents even when they are extremely weak—less than one odor molecule in 1 billion molecules of air. Humans are incredibly good at detecting amyl acetate (the fragrance of bananas).

• Different moods like anger or fear change your personal scent. You aren't aware of it, but when your nose picks up another person's smell, it can influence your emotions and actions.

• Every person has their own signature scent. At only 6 days old, a baby may recognize its mother by her smell.

THE BODY

FEEL THE BEAT FROM

From the soles of your feet
(they're called the plantae pedis)
to the pate on your noggin,
you'd need encyclopedias
if you want to try to log in
all the lame-sounding names
we've made up for our frames,
like your pelvis
(do you know Elvis?),
they include your hips,
the nares (or nostrils),
the vermilion (or lips),
the philtrum, that groove that
comes down in between 'em,
and the membrane that
holds your tongue down—
that's the frenulum.
'Tween your eyebrows,
the glabella;
the pollex is
your thumb;

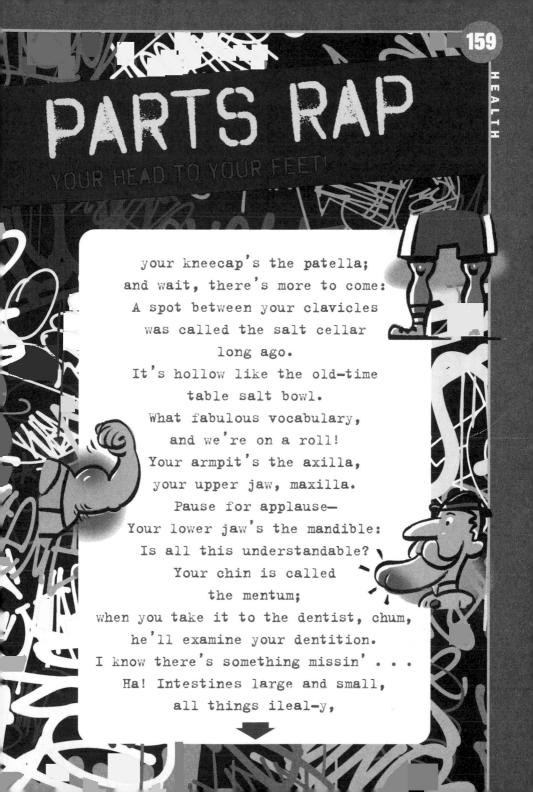

PARTS RAP

YOUR HEAD TO YOUR FEET!

your kneecap's the patella;
and wait, there's more to come:
A spot between your clavicles
was called the salt cellar
long ago.
It's hollow like the old-time
table salt bowl.
What fabulous vocabulary,
and we're on a roll!
Your armpit's the axilla,
your upper jaw, maxilla.
Pause for applause—
Your lower jaw's the mandible:
Is all this understandable?
Your chin is called
the mentum;
when you take it to the dentist, chum,
he'll examine your dentition.
I know there's something missin' . . .
Ha! Intestines large and small,
all things ileal-y,

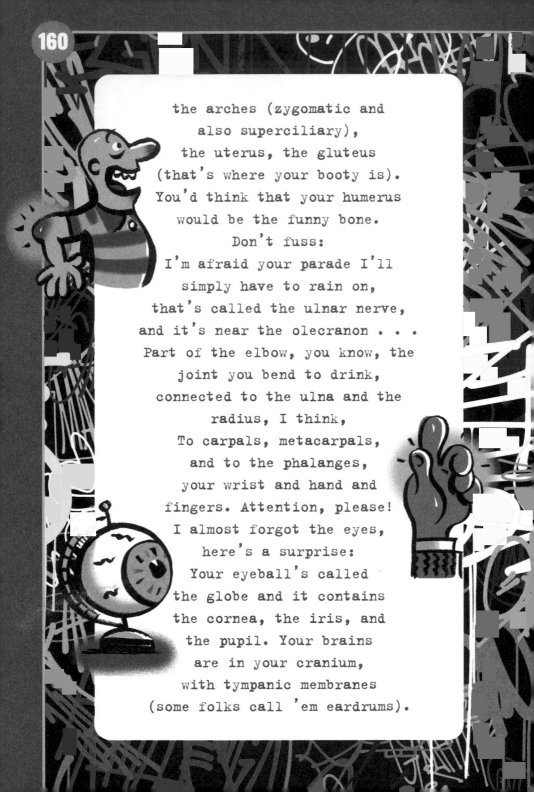

the arches (zygomatic and
also superciliary),
the uterus, the gluteus
(that's where your booty is).
You'd think that your humerus
would be the funny bone.
Don't fuss:
I'm afraid your parade I'll
simply have to rain on,
that's called the ulnar nerve,
and it's near the olecranon . . .
Part of the elbow, you know, the
joint you bend to drink,
connected to the ulna and the
radius, I think,
To carpals, metacarpals,
and to the phalanges,
your wrist and hand and
fingers. Attention, please!
I almost forgot the eyes,
here's a surprise:
Your eyeball's called
the globe and it contains
the cornea, the iris, and
the pupil. Your brains
are in your cranium,
with tympanic membranes
(some folks call 'em eardrums).

Look out! Heads up! Here comes
your ears, with the outer
(called the pinna),
the middle, and the "inna."
Is it time for dinna?
There's more body lore,
we can't ignore the thorax
(that's where your ribs are glued).
If this were a play, we'd have to
have four acts
just to make certain before
the curtain we include
each corner where your
top and bottom eyelids
meet, the canthus.
Yeah! We've got all the "anthuhs"!
Now it's time to thank the
parents who did create us,
but wait! Hesitate! Look up
from your plate,
And give it up for the
external meatus!
That's the ear canal, you
couldn't hear your pal
without it. You'd have
to shout it!
So, we're glad that we had
the time to rhyme about it.

BLOOD

THE **GOOD** AND THE **GROSS**

Your blood is made up of liquid and cells. The liquid part, called plasma, makes up most of your blood. It is a mixture of water, sugar, fat, protein, and salt. The rest is made up of trillions of red blood cells, white blood cells, and cell pieces called platelets.

Each part of your blood has a different job:

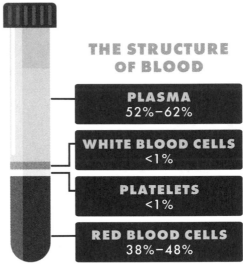

THE STRUCTURE OF BLOOD

PLASMA
52%–62%

WHITE BLOOD CELLS
<1%

PLATELETS
<1%

RED BLOOD CELLS
38%–48%

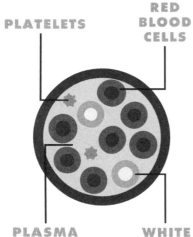

PLATELETS

RED BLOOD CELLS

PLASMA

WHITE BLOOD CELLS

PLASMA transports blood cells throughout your body.

WHITE BLOOD CELLS come in many shapes and sizes and help to protect you from infections and disease.

PLATELETS are colorless cell fragments that clump together to form clots to stop or control bleeding.

RED BLOOD CELLS are indented, disc-shape cells that carry oxygen from your lungs to your tissues and organs and then return carbon dioxide back to the lungs to be exhaled. These cells contain hemoglobin, a protein that gives blood its red color.

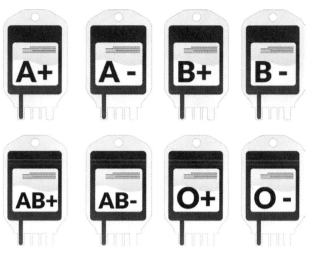

ARE YOU A, B, AB, OR O?

Blood comes in four types—A, B, AB, and O—and contains substances called antigens. Your type is determined by your antigens and your parents' types. If the "Rh factor" protein is present, your type is "positive" with a plus sign after it; if it isn't, you're "negative" with a minus sign. If you ever need a transfusion (blood added to your body), the blood type must be compatible or you will get sick.

AN 80-POUND CHILD HAS NEARLY 6 PINTS OF BLOOD, WHILE AN AVERAGE ADULT HAS BETWEEN 9 AND 12 PINTS.

RED, GREEN, AND CLEAR, TOO!

Although your blood is red, your veins appear blue due to the way that light penetrates and reflects off your skin. But not all blood is red. Several types of **OCTOPUSES** have blue blood. The blood of the ocellated ice fish of Antarctica is clear, and the blood of the **SKINK LIZARD** of New Guinea is green. Flatworms, nematodes, **JELLYFISH,** sea anemones, and corals have no blood at all!

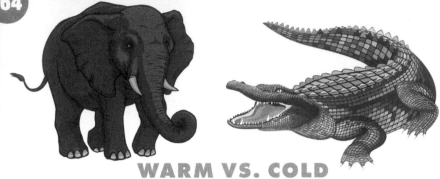

WARM VS. COLD

Humans are called warm-blooded creatures because our internal temperature remains about the same as long as we wear enough clothing and eat enough food. Other mammals and birds are also warm-blooded, growing thick fur or feathers or eating more to stay warm in winter.

The internal temperature of cold-blooded creatures, such as reptiles and amphibians, changes with the outside temperature. Because these creatures rely on sunshine and other heat sources to stay warm, on cool, cloudy days they move slowly and eat less, if at all. When warmed enough on sunny days, they move quickly and hunt for food. In the winter, they bury themselves deep in the mud or sand to survive.

THE EYES HAVE IT!

Tiny horned toads (also called horned lizards) have a unique defense mechanism. If one ends up in the mouth of a predator, it shoots blood from its eyes! This leaves a horrible taste in the predator's mouth and causes it to drop the toad, which quickly escapes.

SCENT-SATIONAL!

Bloodhound dogs can smell and follow the blood trails of animals. Their sense of smell is so remarkable that they also can track people who have gone missing just by sniffing the air and ground. A bloodhound's nose is more accurate than any scenting machine yet invented.

THERE REALLY *IS* A VAMPIRE . . . BAT!

Vampire bats live in Mexico and Central and South America. During their search for food, they use their teeth to make a tiny cut in a large animal, then lap up the blood. The small amount of blood loss does not hurt the animal. Vampire bats do not feed on humans.

A FLOOD OF BLOOD FACTS

- Only female mosquitoes bite. They must drink their body weight in blood in order to lay eggs.
- The bloodroot plant has bright, reddish-orange sap, which Native Americans used for dye.
- Blood pudding isn't pudding at all. It's usually a large sausage stuffed with the cooked blood and fat of pigs.
- A total eclipse of the Moon is sometimes called a Blood Moon because of the Moon's red-orange color.

REACH FOR A LEECH

Bloodsuckers, or leeches, are worms that live in ponds and marshes and dine on the blood of frogs, fish, alligators, and even people. Leeches have been used in medicine for thousands of years because an enzyme in their saliva acts as a blood thinner. At one time, when doctors needed to reconnect veins that had been cut, they attached leeches to drink some of the patient's blood. During this process, saliva introduced from the leech increased blood flow and helped to prevent blood clots until the veins could regrow and circulation be restored.

THE *OTHER* WASHINGTON ZOO

A raccoon, an alligator, a snake—oh, my! Presidents sure have had some peculiar pets!

While many visitors to Washington, D.C., have the good fortune to visit the Smithsonian's National Zoo, few realize that lots of interesting animals have lived at 1600 Pennsylvania Avenue—the White House—over the years. While President Trump did not have any pets, other recent presidents have mostly had dogs and cats. In addition to a cat, President Biden has two German shepherds, Champ and Major, the latter being the first rescue dog to live at the White House. President Obama and his family had two Portuguese water dogs named Bo and Sunny. President George W. Bush had a couple of Scottish terriers, an English springer spaniel, and a cat named Willie. President Bill Clinton had Buddy, a Labrador retriever, and a cat named Socks. But if we go back in history, we find some *unusual* pets.

BILLY, THE OPOSSUM

President Herbert Hoover had an opossum called Billy. He was a wild opossum that had strayed onto the White House grounds. The Hoovers took a liking to him and built him a pen outside. A high school in nearby Maryland borrowed Billy to serve as a mascot for their sports teams. He was returned to the White House after they won many sports awards.

THE ALLIGATOR

President John Quincy Adams received an alligator as a gift from a French general. It stayed in a bathtub in the unfinished East Room of the White House. The president enjoyed showing the gator to visitors.

Wash.

PETE, THE SQUIRREL

President Warren Harding had two dogs and many canaries, but he also had a pet gray squirrel named Pete, who often took walks with the president and could be seen running through the halls of the White House. Sometimes Pete dropped in on press conferences and news briefings!

REBECCA, THE RACCOON

President Calvin Coolidge had so many pets that the White House was sometimes called The Pennsylvania Avenue Zoo. A raccoon was sent to the president to be part of the Thanksgiving meal, but the Coolidges found the raccoon to be very friendly and kept her as a pet. They named her Rebecca. She lived in a large tree outside the president's office. When she was indoors, she liked to play in the bathtub with water and a bar of soap.

Spotty's Spot in History

In 1989, Millie, President George H. W. Bush's family dog, had a litter of puppies at the White House. One of the pups, Spotty, became the pet of future president George W. Bush. Spotty is said to be the first pet to have lived in the White House twice.

OLD IKE, THE RAM

President Woodrow Wilson had a flock of sheep that grazed on the White House lawn, led by a ram called Old Ike. Their fleece was sold to raise money for the American Red Cross. Old Ike was not a very nice pet. He chased White House staff and police and chewed any discarded cigars he could find.

OLD WHISKERS, THE GOAT

President Benjamin Harrison had a goat named Old Whiskers, which often pulled the Harrison grandchildren around the White House lawn in a cart. One day, Old Whiskers took off with a grandchild in the cart. He exited the White House gates and headed down the street. The president set off running after the goat and caught the cart just before it hit a ditch.

EMILY SPINACH, THE SNAKE

President Theodore Roosevelt owned many untraditional pets, such as two kangaroo rats and a badger. His oldest daughter, Alice, had a pet garter snake that she carried around in her purse and showed off at unexpected times. Sometimes she hid it under a plate during dinner! Alice said that she named the snake Emily Spinach because it was as thin as her Aunt Emily and as green as spinach.

Prime Ministers' Pets
THE THREE PATS

Canada's 10th prime minister, William Lyon Mackenzie King, loved dogs. He received an Irish terrier from a friend and named him Pat. He praised Pat as "a God-sent little angel in the guise of a dog." Later he had two more Irish terriers, both also named Pat! He often talked and read to his dogs and asked them for advice.

STANLEY, GYPSY, AND CHARLIE

Stephen Harper, who was Canada's 22nd prime minister, is very fond of cats. Stanley and Gypsy, both cats, and a chinchilla named Charlie all lived at the prime minister's residence in Ottawa when he was in office. The Harper family also foster-homed dozens of cats and other small animals before they were ready to be adopted. After a fire destroyed an animal shelter, they took in 11 kittens.

Dog Heaven

Queen Elizabeth II of England is also the queen regnant of Canada. She has owned more than 30 Pembroke Welsh corgis during her reign. She received her first corgi, Susan, on her 18th birthday. The dogs have all lived in Buckingham Palace in a special Corgi Room, which is filled with elevated wicker baskets covered with sheets that are changed daily. All of the dogs' meals are prepared fresh by a personal chef. At Christmas, the queen gifts each dog with toys and goodies.

CALMING Creatures

SOMETIMES SPENDING TIME WITH AN ANIMAL CAN HELP A PERSON TO FEEL BETTER. THESE ANIMALS PROVE THAT THEY HAVE WHAT IT TAKES TO HELP OTHERS.

A PIG With Personality

My name is Lilou. I am a 5-year-old miniature painted pig.
I am proud to be known as the world's first animal therapy pig.

MY STORY: I was born in Michigan and moved to San Francisco as a piglet. In pig years, I'm a young adult. I eat only organic vegetables and vegetarian protein pellets. Yum!

HOW I HELP: I calm nervous travelers at the San Francisco airport and visit nursing homes and hospitals. People pet me, shake my hoof, and take selfies with me. I can stand on my back hooves and twirl, plus I play a toy piano with my hooves and snout.

MY TRAINING: I was certified as an Animal-Assisted Therapist at the San Francisco Society for the Prevention of Cruelty to Animals. I am part of the airport's "Wag Brigade," along with my dog friends Brixton, Jagger, and Toby.

I LOVE wearing costumes—especially my blue tutu, pilot's cap, and "Pet Me!" vest. And I adore getting my "hooficure," when nontoxic red polish is painted on my toenails.

Something to CROW About

My name is Winston Bontempo, and I am the world's first therapy rooster. I'm a 4-year-old Malaysian Serama chicken, the smallest chicken breed in the world. I stand less than 10 inches from my shoulder to the ground—half the size of most of my relatives.

MY STORY: I was hatched on a small farm in Ohio and live there with the Bontempo family. As a young chick, I bonded with people, and my human mom began to take me to garden shows and flea markets. The response from people was so positive that she decided that I would make a perfect therapy rooster. And now I am!

HOW I HELP: I regularly visit the Cleveland Medical Clinic and Veterans' Hospital, where I sit on people's laps so that they can hug and cuddle me. My catlike purr has a calming effect.

MY TRAINING was done at the West Geauga Veterinary Hospital in Chesterland, Ohio, where I proved that I could behave myself around people, with no pecking or scratching ever. The Cleveland Medical Clinic sent me a letter praising my therapeutic skills.

I LOVE getting dressed up for visits in my homemade red bandanna. It makes me feel handsome. Being a rooster, I love to crow, although the sound that I make is much softer than that of my larger relatives.

Good-Hearted GOATS

Hello! I'm Jasper! My friend Zephyr and I are pygmy therapy goats. We measure about 16 inches from our shoulders to the ground. Our ancestors came from the nation of Cameroon in West Africa, which is why we are called Cameroon Dwarf Goats.

OUR STORY: We were born at Griffiths Pygmy Farm in Meadow Vista, California, and completed our therapy training there. When a family came to the farm looking for a therapy goat for their son, they decided to adopt both Zephyr and me. Now we live on another farm, where our new owner's son visits us almost daily.

HOW WE HELP: Zephyr and I are calm and quiet with our new friend. We let him do all the talking, and if he wants to read to us, we listen. Our new friend's reading and social skills have improved since we came into his life.

OUR TRAINING: The Griffith family trained us when we were kids. They gave us lots of love and attention and taught us to remain calm no matter the situation. We are quiet and gentle goats.

WE LOVE to play, run, jump into the air, and chase each other around. But spending time with our friend is what we love most.

Amazing ALPACA

Hi! My name is Brando's Napoleon. I am related to llamas, but I am smaller and have straighter ears and a flatter face. My closest relatives came from the Andes mountains of Peru in South America.

MY STORY: I live at Mountain Peaks Therapy Llamas and Alpacas in Washington state and am their first certified therapy alpaca. When I was a cria, or baby alpaca, my caretakers saw that I enjoyed being with humans and liked to go out on my own. They knew that I had what it took to help people.

HOW I HELP: I visit senior facilities, elementary schools, and children's hospitals. I stand quietly while people hug me and touch my soft fleece. I know that I'm doing a good job when I see them smile.

MY TRAINING was done at the Dove Lewis Animal Hospital. When I met people, I was respectful and calm—even when someone pulled too hard on my fleece!

I LOVE to dress up for parades and fashion shows (I'm a model!). Sometimes I meet celebrities and have photographs taken with them! My human moms like to make sweaters from my fleece, and that makes me happy.

DO YOU SEE IT?

You're sitting down for lunch with a hot bowl of soup and suddenly notice something strange: Your soup is staring back at you! Or at least it looks that way.

You are experiencing pareidolia (pear-eye-DOE-lee-a)—a fancy word meaning that you see a recognizable object or pattern in an unrelated object or pattern.

Look at these pictures and see if anything seems familiar to you. Ask your family and friends what they see. Can you find any examples of pareidolia in your home or neighborhood?

AMUSEMENT

"EIGENGRAU"* IS THE "COLOR" YOU SEE WHEN YOU OPEN YOUR EYES IN A COMPLETELY DARK ROOM.
*pronounced EYEg-n-grau—the last part rhymes with "how"!

AMAZING AND TRUE!

ASTOUND YOUR FRIENDS, FAMILY, AND TEACHERS WITH THESE MIND-BOGGLING FACTS!

One little brown bat can eat 1,000 mosquitoes in an hour!

Honeybees must visit about 2 million flowers to make 1 pound of honey!

A HILL IN NEW ZEALAND HAS THE LONGEST PLACE NAME ON EARTH!

Taumatawhakatangihangakoauauotamateaturipukakapikimaungahoronukupokaiwhenuakitanatahu.
It means: "place where Tamatea, the man with the big knees, who slid, climbed, and swallowed mountains, known as 'Land-eater,' played his flute to his loved one."

The world's first underwater mailbox, in Susami Bay, Japan, is about 33 feet underwater. Thirty-two thousand pieces of mail have been posted from it since its installation!

THE DISTANCE BETWEEN ALASKA AND RUSSIA IS ONLY 55 MILES!

A 100-pound giant Pacific octopus can squeeze itself through a hole the size of an orange!

Humans and giraffes have the same number of vertebrae in their neck: seven!

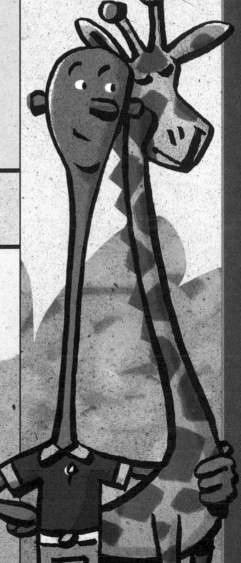

THE ONLY NUMBER WITH ITS LETTERS IN ALPHABETICAL ORDER WHEN SPELLED OUT IS 40 (F-O-R-T-Y)!

Southernmost Canada (Middle Island, Ontario) is south of northernmost Pennsylvania!

IN NORTH CAROLINA ON THE FIRST SUNDAY OF NOVEMBER 2007, the Cirioli twins were born: Peter at 1:32 A.M. and then, 34 minutes later, Allison. However, because Daylight Saving Time reverted to Standard Time at 2:00 A.M. that day, Allison was officially born at 1:06 A.M., thus becoming her older brother's older sister!

The largest water lily in the world, *Victoria amazonica*, grows leaves up to 10 feet in diameter!

A single aurora borealis (northern lights) display can produce 1 trillion watts of electricity!

WHAT ARE YOU AFRAID OF?

pho·bi·a   FOE-be-a   *noun*

1. A phobia is a persistent, abnormal, or irrational fear of a specific thing or situation that compels one to avoid the feared stimulus.

2. A phobia is also strong fear, dislike, or aversion.

PHOBIA SUBJECT	PHOBIA TERM
Animals	Zoophobia
Beards	Pogonophobia
Birds	Ornithophobia
Blood	Hematophobia
Choking	Pnigophobia
Crossing bridges	Gephyrophobia
Crowds	Ochlophobia
Dreams	Oneirophobia
Flowers	Anthophobia
Flying	Aerophobia
Garlic	Alliumphobia
Germs	Mysophobia
Haircuts	Tonsurephobia
Height	Acrophobia
Height, being near something of great	Batophobia
Hospitals	Nosocomephobia
Illness	Nosemaphobia
Lakes	Limnophobia
Lightning and thunder	Astraphobia
Long words	Sesquipedalophobia
Men	Androphobia
Money	Chrometophobia

PHOBIA SUBJECT	PHOBIA TERM
Night, darkness	Nyctophobia
Open or public places	Agoraphobia
Shadows	Sciophobia
Snakes	Ophidiophobia
Sun	Heliophobia
Touch	Haphephobia
Trains and train travel	Siderodromophobia
Water	Hydrophobia
Women	Gynophobia

What's the Title?
Use the alphabet below to decode.

____ ____ ____ ____ ____ ____ ____ ____

Sign language is a way to communicate without using your voice. It involves using your hands, body posture, and facial expressions. Although sign language is used mostly by people who are deaf or can't hear well, it can be used by anyone. There are even animals that use sign language. A gorilla named Koko learned more than 1,000 signs! In North America, we use American Sign Language, but there are different versions across the world.

Using the alphabet below, spell your name.
Then teach a friend to spell their name.

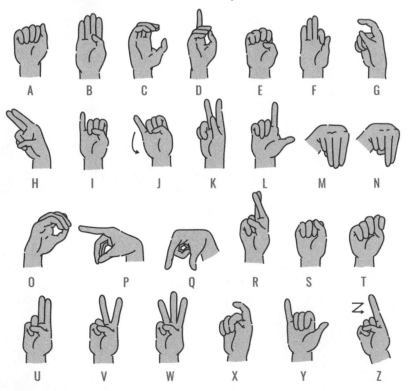

Here are some common signs and phrases to get you started in your new language adventure.

HELLO: Open your hand with all of your fingers pointing up and your thumb crossed in front of your palm. Touch the side of your forehead, then quickly move your hand away from your head.

GOOD-BYE: Open your palm, fold down your fingers, then open your palm again. Repeat once or twice.

YES: Make an "S" sign and bend your wrist forward like you are nodding "yes."

NO: Open and close your index and middle finger over your thumb twice.

FAMILY: Make an "F" sign with each hand, palms facing out, with thumbs touching. Move your hands away from each other, making a circle in front of you. End with the backs of your hands facing out.

SORRY: Make an "S" sign and rub your chest in a circular motion toward your shoulder.

I LOVE YOU: With your palm facing out, hold up your thumb, index finger, and pinky.

LOVE: Make a fist with each hand and cross your arms over your chest.

PLEASE: Open your hand and rub your chest in a circular motion.

THANK YOU: Open your hand and touch your chin with your fingertips. Move the hand away from you.

HOW A COMIC STRIP IS MADE

EVERY ARTIST HAS A UNIQUE WAY OF WORKING. KELLY ALDER TAKES YOU BEHIND THE SCENES TO SHOW YOU HOW HE CREATED THE COMIC STRIP ON **PAGES 146–151**. IT'S A LOT MORE WORK THAN YOU MIGHT THINK!

STAGE 1: THUMBNAILS

This stage is a first pass—a quick, rough breakdown of how I want to tell the story and lay out the pages and the panels. I work fast and loose so that when I have to make revisions, I haven't spent a lot of time on the first pass.

"I've always liked to draw. And, not surprisingly, I've always loved reading comics! Whether they were in book form from the store or in the newspaper, they influenced me in how and what I drew."

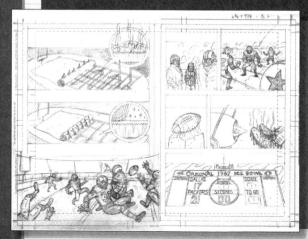

STAGE 2: PENCILS

After I've discussed the thumbnails with the art director, he or she shows them to the editor. Then the art director and I talk about what is good and what might need to be changed. I use this feedback to make changes and then tighten up my sketches. In this case, I needed to revise the bottom panels on these pages.

STAGE 3: INKS

After tightening and cleaning up my pencil sketches come the inks. I use special pens to create the panels and the images within them. Many illustrators

and comic book artists do all of their inking digitally, but I still prefer to do mine by hand. Then I scan the inks and clean up smudges and any mistakes in a program called Photoshop.

STAGE 4: COLOR

I do the next step in layers, again using Photoshop. First, I separate the ink lines from the white background and put them on their own layer. I make a new layer underneath the inks

and apply flat colors throughout the page. I duplicate the flat color layer and use it to apply several techniques that add texture and dimension to the illustration.

Finally, after the art director and I select a typeface
that's appropriate, the art director digitally places the words
in the panels with another program called InDesign.

The whole process is a collaboration between the
editor, art director, and me. In this case, we had a great team,
which made for a fun and rewarding experience!

TABLE OF MEASURES

LENGTH/DISTANCE

1 foot = 12 inches
1 yard = 3 feet = 0.914 meter
1 meter = 39.37 inches
1 mile = 1,760 yards = 5,280 feet =
 1.61 kilometers
1 kilometer = 0.62 mile

AREA

1 square inch = 6.45 square
 centimeters
1 square foot = 144 square inches
1 square yard = 9 square feet = 0.84
 square meter
1 acre = 43,560 square feet = 0.40
 hectare
1 hectare = 2.47 acres
1 square mile = 640 acres = 2.59
 square kilometers
1 square kilometer = 0.386 square mile

HOUSEHOLD
(approx. equivalents)

½ teaspoon = 2.5 mL
1 teaspoon = 5 mL
3 teaspoons = 1 tablespoon = 15 mL
¼ cup = 60 mL
⅓ cup = 75 mL
½ cup = 120 mL
¾ cup = 175 mL
1 cup = 16 tablespoons = 8 ounces =
 240 mL
2 liquid cups = 1 pint = 0.5 liter
2 liquid pints = 1 quart = 1 liter
4 liquid quarts = 1 gallon = 4 liters

SPEED/VELOCITY
(mph = miles per hour;
kph = kilometers per hour)

1 mph = 1.609 kph
1 knot = 1.15 mph = 1.85 kph

COMPARE CELSIUS AND FAHRENHEIT

To convert Celsius and Fahrenheit

$$°C = (°F - 32) / 1.8 \quad \blacksquare \quad °F = (°C \times 1.8) + 32$$

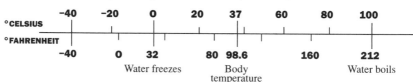

°CELSIUS	-40	-20	0	20	37	60	80	100
°FAHRENHEIT	-40	0	32		80 98.6		160	212

Water freezes | Body temperature | Water boils

COMPARE INCHES TO CENTIMETERS

1 inch = 2.54 centimeters
1 centimeter = 0.39 inch

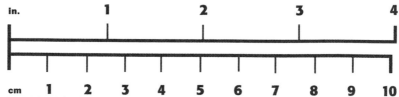

SOLUTIONS TO GAMES AND PUZZLES

"The Halloween Hunt" on page 23

"Travel Unravel" on page 63

"Digging for Garden Words" on page 89

"Treasure Hunt" on page 117

"Penguin Pucks" on page 145

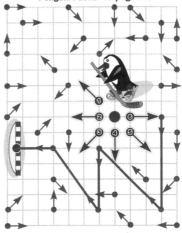

ACKNOWLEDGMENTS

PICTURE CREDITS

ABBREVIATIONS:
FB—Facebook
GI—Getty Images
NASA—National Aeronautics and Space Administration
PX—Pixabay
SS—Shutterstock
WM—Wikimedia
WP—Wikipedia
Front Cover: dennisvdw/GI
Back Cover: chicagobulls.com (Michael Jordan). DFree/SS (Billie Eilish). Zocha_K/GI (frog). dottedhippo/GI (Pluto). YouTube.com (ice apple). Kelly Alder (comic). Diane Kuhl/GI (cows). VOOK/SS (puzzle).
Front Matter: 1: Kelly Alder. 2: Leonard Zhukovsky/SS (top). nikpal/GI (center top). Erhan Inga/SS (center bottom). Bigandt_Photography/GI (bottom). 3: flaticon.com (top icons). akinbostanci/GI (question marks).
Calendar: 8: NASA (Rover). Walt Disney (Mickey Mouse). WM (President Obama). WM (Wayne Gretzky). Gage_Skidmore/WP (Justin Timberlake). 9: Amazon.com (Tom Brady). NASA (Moon). scott mecum/WP (Steve Nash). Kasio69/WP (Rihanna). lunewind/GI (snow background). 10: vladimir_karpenyuk/GI (snowflakes background). Grahampurse/WM (Yellowstone National Park). Sergiozaragoza/WM (Fernando Iglesias). Keith Hinkle/WP (Carrie Underwood). Britannica.com (Marc Garneau). Angela George/WM (Brenda Song). 11: GARY GERSHOFF (Skai Jackson). TheGuardian.com (Terry Fox). Julio Enriquez/WM (Chance the Rapper). Marc Piscotty/WM (Kelly Clarkson). 12: KnowYourMeme.com (Dwayne Johnson). Scott Davis/Bigfoot 911 (Bigfoot). FB/kentucky derby (Kentucky Derby). wikiwand (Daniel Goodwin). Stock Store/SS (marlin). 13: GlobalP/GI (bald eagle). chicagobulls.com (Michael Jordan). Ken Maynard/WP (Venus Williams). Fandom (Garfield the Cat). Claire_Leahy/WM (Mindy Kaling). Simone Castrovillari/SwimSwam.com (Michael Phelps). 14: Pobytov/GI (meadow background). pamela_d_mcadams/GI (french fries). Condé Nast Traveler (Disneyland). WP (Selena Gomez). Eva Rinaldi (Bindi Irwin). WM (Bill Mueller). 15: Kathy Hutchins (Dylan and Cole Sprouse). Walt Disney (Donald Duck). subjug/GI (s'mores). Jeff McIntosh CP (Cindy Klassen). hamilton.com (Aretha Franklin). myblackhistory.net (Althea Gibson). 16: 4khz/GI (rain background). Sassy/WM (Beyoncé). Pittsburgh Zoo (rhino). gdcgraphics/WP (Alexis Bledel). FB (Cal Ripken Jr.). TechCrunch/WM (Will Smith). 17: Gage Skidmore/WM (Noah Schnapp). motivationalspeakers.ca (Laurie Skreslet). s_bukley/SS (Bruno Mars). RuthBlack/GI (cupcake). subjug/GI (ice cream). greg2600/WM (Katy Perry). swimswam.com (Amanda Beard). 18: Amazon.com (Jacques Plante). WM (football). kidscreen.com (Sesame Street). Aubrey Gemignani/WM (Ryan Gosling). Parkerjh/WM (David Ortiz). Gage_Skidmore/WM (Scarlett Johansson). 19: NASA (pizza party). holyrosaryparish.org (Marguerite d'Youville). DFree/SS (Billie Eilish). Walt Disney (Snow White). Fernando Frazão/Agência Brasil/WM (Gabby Douglas). 20: kutaytanir/GI (top right). ttsz/GI (center). Anastasiia Okhrimenko/GI (center left). Anastasiia_M/GI (bottom left). 21: Alexandrum79/GI (center). Diversity Studio/GI (bottom right). 22: duncan1890/GI (top). smartboy10/GI (bottom). 23: Igor Zakowski/GI. 24–26: stellalevi/GI (background). 24: LumiNola/GI. 25: fizkes/GI (top right). aldomurillo/GI (center left). SDI Productions/GI (center right). CREATISTA/GI (bottom). 26: Imgorthand/GI (center left). kate_sept2004/GI (center right). 27: ratselmeister/SS.
Astronomy: 28: dottedhippo/GI (center). NASA (bottom right). 30: J. Weston & Son Photographers. 31: Ekkalak Ngamjarasvanij/SS (background). 32–37: Tim Robinson (illustrations). 38: NASA. 39: NASA.

Weather: 40–45 Vector/GI (background). 40: Hulinska_Yevheniia/GI (bottom). 41: PiccoloNamek/WP (top right). klyaksun/GI (center). Flagstafffotos/WP (bottom left). UCAR Center for Science Education (bottom middle). Sara Nabih/WP (bottom right). 42: VectorMine/GI. 43: Courtney Devlin. 44: Samantha Bailey/GI (top). JrGarcia/GI (bottom). 45: klyaksun/GI (center). illo myillo/GI (bottom). 46–47: ONYXprj/SS (background). 48–49: simplycmb/iStock. 50–53: Dimitris66/GI (snowflake background). 50: YouTube.com (top). TallyHo Films Inc/SS (center). johannes-plenio unsplash (bottom). 51: NOAA (top). LeManna/GI (bottom). 52: Metrarail/Instagram (top). passion4nature/GI (bottom). 53: amusingplanet.com. 54–55: Jacob Jarvela (illustrations).

On the Farm: 56–57: Diane Kuhl/GI. 58: Diane Kuhl/GI (top). jcyoung2/GI (bottom). 59: AscentXmedia/GI (top). memoangeles/GI (bottom). 60: lukaves/GI (bottom). 61: Clara Bastian/GI (top). ChristinLola/GI (bottom). 62: Irish Farmers Journal (top left). Guinness World Records (top right). 63: VOOK/SS. 64–65: Ksuksa/GI. 66: ChristiLaLiberte/GI (top). miteemaus5/GI (bottom). 67: happyborder/GI (top). Fotokate/GI (bottom). 68: TrudySlinger/GI (top). Bigandt_Photography/GI (bottom). 69: Vera_Petrunina/GI (top). Julia_Siomuh/GI (bottom).

In the Garden: 70: Lowes (bottom). 71–73: Donna Griffith. 74–77: MrsWilkins/GI (background). 74: Cwieders/GI. 75: Paul Reeves Photography/SS. 76: marcophotos/GI. (top left). dvarg/GI (bottom). 77: dvarg/GI (top left). Darryl Saffer/GI (top right). GarysFRP/GI (center left). dvarg/GI (bottom). 78–79: fabian cho/GI. 80: EdwardSamuelCornwall/GI (top). Halfpoint/GI (center). PatrikStedrak/GI (bottom). 81: caribbeangardenseed.com (bottom left). W. Atlee Burpee & Co. (bottom middle). magicgardenseeds.com (bottom right). 82: Becky Luigart-Stayner (center). Brooklyn Museum (bottom). 83: nutriouslife.com (center). kazmulka/GI (bottom). 84: Olga_Mallari/GI (top). studiocasper/GI (bottom).

85: MahirAtes/GI (top). Floortje/GI (bottom). 86: chengyuzheng/GI (top). Nipapornnan/GI (bottom). 87: EHStock/GI (top). Furtseff/GI (center). 88: Jacob Jarvela (illustrations). 89: YZm/SS.

Nature: 90–91: Freder/GI. 92: Evgeny555/GI (top left). WLDavies/GI (top middle). SunRay BRI Cattery RU/GI (top right). Freder/GI (center). nico_blue/GI (bottom). 93: Freder/GI (top). Dominique-Grosse/GI (center). Dptro/GI (bottom). 94: zemkooo/GI (top right). dennis glosik/GI (top left). 95: Martin Mecnarowski/SS (jaguar). JackF/GI (leopard). GlobalP/GI (lion). Puttachat Kumkrong/GI (tiger). clarst5/SS (snow leopard). 96–97: Lindsay Forcino. 98–101: U.S. Fish and Wildlife Service. 102–103: Zocha_K/GI. 104–107: 1 daikokuebisu/GI (background). 104: reptiles4all/GI (top). Azureus70/GI (bottom left). mantella nikpal/GI (bottom right). 105: kikkerdirk/GI (top). Uwe-Bergwitz/GI (center). Thorsten Spoerlein/GI (bottom). 106: Bimbimkha007/GI. 107: MarinaVorontsova/GI. 108: Iamyai/GI. 109: Focus_on_Nature/GI (top). PX (bottom). 110: PX (top left). jganz/GI (top right). PX (center). PX (bottom left). arnoaltix/GI (bottom right). 111: Sarah Perreault.

Awesome Achievers: 113: AGE Fotostock. 114: The Guardian. 115: Nature Conservancy of Canada. 116: Murray State University. 117: Mila_Ludmila/SS. 118–125: Betelgejze/GI (background). 120: FB. 121: YouTube.com. 122: FB. 123: Instagram. 124: National Park Trust. 125: greenteamsuperheroes.com.

Food: 126–129: ElenaMedvedeva/GI (background). 126: Marat Musabırov/GI (top). 127: Tim UR/GI (bottom). 128: Diana Taliun/GI (top). saschanti/GI (bottom). 129: minadezhda/SS. 130: bhofack2/GI (top left). cokada/GI (top right). yipengge/GI (bottom). 131: pulses.org (top). subodhsathe/GI (center left). thesomegirl/GI (center right). Paul_Brighton/GI (bottom). 132: Jupiterimage /GI (top). PicturePartners/GI (center top). Andrei Kravtsov/GI (center bottom). Sara_Winter/GI (bottom). 133: semiseriouschefs.com (top). AnnaPustynnikova/GI (center left). letty17/GI (center right). ALEAIMAGE/GI (bottom). 134: weelicious.com. 135: cookidoo.co.uk. 136: Erhan Inga/SS. 137: Hidden Valley Ranch (top). sherisilver.com (bottom). **Sports:** 138–139: Leonard Zhukovsky/SS. 140: berlingske.dk (top). SMILEY N POOL HC staff (center). Leonard Zhukovsky/SS (bottom). 141: Bill Mallon (top). WP (bottom). 142: apu.fi (top). olympic.org (center). sportsnspokes.com (bottom). 143: WP (top). Leonard Zhukovsky/SS (center top, center, and bottom). 144: Jamaican Bobsled Federation (center right). olympic.ca (center). 145: ratselmeister/SS. 146–151: Kelly Alder. 153: ebay.com (top). YouTube.com (center). **Health:** 154: AaronAmat/GI. 155: Kastoluza/SS. 156: Agustiawan/GI (top). Thinkstock (center). 157: nmaxfield/ GI (bottom). 158–161: Tim Robinson (illustrations). 162: ShadeDesign/SS (top and bottom). 163: jauhari1/GI (top). sceka/GI (bottom left). Bullet_Chained/GI (bottom middle). Bohdanochka/GI (bottom right). 164: subhandworks/GI (top left). ElenaMichaylova/GI (top right). sigonee/ GI (bottom left). Apilart/GI (bottom right). 165: Alfmaler/SS (top left and right). Elena Abramovich/GI (bottom). **Pets:** 166–169: paseven/GI (background). 166: Library of Congress. 167: Library of Congress (top and center). WP (bottom). 168: Library of Congress (top and bottom). 169: VirtualMuseum.ca (top). Heavy.com (center). Pinterest (bottom). 170: FB. 171: Breanna Kulkin. 172: abcnewsgo.com. 173: FB. **Amusement:** 174: Sarah Perreault (top). DG Stock/SS (center left). GSLstudio/GI (center right). Frank Cornelissen/GI (bottom). 175: crisserbug/GI (top). Fabricio Burbano/GI (center left). jessica manavella/GI (center right). Torii Lynn Weaver/SS (bottom). 176–178: Tim Robinson (illustrations). 179: max-kegfire/GI. 180–181: Antonov Maxim/SS. 182–185: Kelly Alder. 187: Igor Zakowski/ GI (top). VOOK/SS (center left). YZm/SS (center right). Mila_Ludmila/SS (bottom left). ratselmeister/SS (bottom right).

CONTRIBUTORS

Kelly Alder: How a Comic Strip Is Made. **Derrick Barnes:** The Pine Tar Incident, excerpted from *Who Got Game? Baseball: Amazing But True Stories!* (2020), used with permission from Workman Publishing. **Bob Berman:** Behold the "Supermoon"! **Emma Biggs:** Pots That Rock!, excerpted from *Gardening With Emma* (2019), used with permission from Storey Publishing. **Christopher Burnett:** Dynamic Dart Frogs. **Jack Burnett:** Frozen Football: The Ice Bowl. **Alice Cary:** So, You Want to Live in Space?, Look What I Found!, Environmental Warriors, Games of Glory: All About the Olympics. **Tim Clark:** The Astronaut Who Was Allergic to the Moon, How Cold *Was* It?, The Body Parts Rap. **Janet Dohner:** Old MacDonald Had a Dog. **Stephanie Gibeault:** Perplexing Pluto's Planet Status, Know Your Nose. **Mare-Anne Jarvela:** Cows and Moos, Who Put the "Straw" in Strawberries?, The *Other* Washington Zoo. **Benjamin Kilbride:** Make Way for Duck Stamps. **Barbara Lassonde:** Blood: The Good and the Gross. **Martie Majoros:** Garden Snack Attack. **Sheryl Normandeau:** Eyes on the Skies for Dragonflies! **Sarah Perreault:** What Happened in History?, Cracking the Coconut, Breakfast Around the World, Fun and Flavorful!, Do You See It?, Sign Here. **Heidi Stonehill:** The Big Cats. **Robin Sweetser:** Meet the Humble Bumble. **Carol Watson:** Kindness Is Contagious!, Calming Creatures.

Content not cited here is adapted from *The Old Farmer's Almanac* archives or appears in the public domain. Every effort has been made to attribute all material correctly. If any errors have been unwittingly committed, they will be corrected in a future edition.

INDEX

ACTIVITIES

Big Cat Match Game, 94
Cow Quiz, 62
Craft Some Pinecone Critters, 96–97
Create Your Own Colorful Frogs, 106–107
DIY Dragonfly, 111
Grow Some Strawberries, 80
Grow Trash-Can Potatoes, 88
Hypertufa How-to, 72–73
Kindness Day Actions, 24–26
Make a Cloud in a Jar, 43
Make Some Frubbles, 50

Pareidolia, 174–175
Plant a Bumblebee Buffet, 76
Plant a Snack Garden, 84–87
Puzzles
  Digging for Garden Words, 89
  Mirrored Twins, 27
  Penguin Pucks, 145
  Solutions to Games and Puzzles, 187
  The Halloween Hunt, 23
  Travel Unravel, 63
  Treasure Hunt, 117

Recipes
  Baked potato mice, 135
  Banana sushi, 134
  Coconut banana smoothie, 128
  Coconut oatmeal cookies, 129
  Owl s'mores, 137
  Pizza faces, 137
  Strawberry lemonade, 82
  Tropical fruit trees, 136
Sign Language, 180–181
Weather Tracker, 47

A
Archaeological team, 114
Archaeologist, 112
Astronauts, 32–37, 38–39

B
Baseball, 152–153
Blood, 162–165
Bluetooth, origin of, 112
Body, the human
  Blood, 162–165
  Nose, 154–157
  Parts of the, 158–161
Breakfasts, international 130–133
Brett, George, 152–153
Bumblebees, 74–77
Burney, Venetia, 30

C
Calendar Pages, monthly
  January, 8
  February, 9
  March, 10
  April, 11
  May, 12
  June, 13
  July, 14
  August, 15
  September, 16
  October, 17
  November, 18

December, 19
Cats
  "Big," 90–95
  Cheetahs, 92
  Cougars, 92
  Jaguar, 92–95
  Leopards, 92–95
  Liger, 93
  "Small," 55 (house), 92, 93
  Snow leopards, 92–95
  Tiger, 91–95
  Tigon, 93
Cernan, Gene, 38
Clouds, 40–45, 46
Coconuts, 126–129
Comic strip, how it's made, 182–185
Cows, 55, 56–62

D
Day(s)
  Kindness Day, 24
  Week, origin of a, 20–22
Dogs, 64–69
  Bloodhound, 164
  Border collie, 64, 67
  Cairn terrier, 68
  Corgis, 67, 169
  German shepherd, 67
  Great Pyrenees, 66
  Herding, 67
  Hunting, 68

Irish terrier, 169
Italian Maremma, 66
Leonberger, 69
Livestock guardian, 66
Multipurpose, 69
Newfoundland, 69
Rat terrier, 68
Dragonflies, 108–111
Duck stamps, 98–101

F
Facts, Amazing, 176–178
Football, 146–151
Fossils, hadrosaur, 115
Foxes, 55
Frogs, poison dart, 102–105

H
Home remedies
  Coconut oil, 127
  Strawberry bath, 82
  Strawberry face mask, 83
  Strawberry sunburn soother, 83
  Strawberry toothpaste, 83
Horses, 55

I
Ice
  Apples, 50
  Balls, 48–49
  Bubbles, 50

Football game, 146–151
Pancake, 51
Volcanoes, 53
Insects
Ants, 54
Bees, 54, 74–77
Dragonflies, 108–110
Hornets, 55
Mosquitoes, 165
Treehoppers, 116

J

Jellyfish, 163

K

Kids
Beckers, Sylvie, 116
Biggs, Emma, 70–73
Bowles, Stella, 120
Burke, Trevor, 121
Green Team Superheroes, 125
Hrushkin, Nathan, 115
Lin, Audrey, 122
Malaschnitschenko, Luca, 112–113
Moralevitz, Ryan, 123
Stamp, Joslyn, 124
Thunberg, Greta, 118–119
Vanecek, Saga, 114

L

Leeches (bloodsuckers), 165
Lizards
Horned toads, 164
Iguanas, 52
Skink, 163

M

Measures, Table of, 186
Metal detector, 112
Metric conversion, 186
Milk, 58, 59, 61
Moon
dust, 38–39
names, 8–19, 165
super, 31

N

Nose, 154–157

O

Octopuses, 163, 177

Olympians
Biles, Simone, 143
Comaneci, Nadia, 143
Connolly, James, 141
Guttmann, Ludwig, 142
Jamaican bobsledders, 144
Kim, Chloe, 139, 140
Kirvesniemi-Hämäläinen, Marja-Liisa, 142
Lemieux, Lawrence, 144
Lipinski, Tara, 140
Loundras, Dimitrios, 140
Nishida, Shuhei, 141
Oe, Sueo, 141
Sørensen, Inge, 140
Olympics
Events, 140–144
Games' origin, 138
Medals, 142
Paralympic Games, 142
Torch, 144

P

Paleontology, 115
Pareidolia, 174–175
Pets
Alligator, 166
Alpaca, 173
Canaries, 167
Cats, 169
Dogs, 166, 167, 169
Goats, 168, 172
Opossum, 166
Pig, miniature painted, 170
Raccoon, 167
Ram, 168
Rooster, 171
Sheep, 168
Snake, 168
Squirrel, 167
Therapeutic, 170–173
Phobias, 179
Plants (flowers)
Bee balm, 76
Black-eyed Susans, 76
California poppies, 76
Coneflowers, 76
Crocuses, 76
Hellebore, 76
Larkspur, 76
Lungwort, 76
Phlox, 76

Salvia, 76
Spring ephemerals, 76
Sunflowers, 76, 87
Virginia bluebells, 76
Wild geranium, 76
Plants (edibles)
Basil, 76
Chives, 76
Cilantro, 76
Edamame, 86
Ground cherries, 85
Parsley, 76
Potatoes, 88
Snap peas, 84
Strawberries, 80
Sunflower seeds, 87
Pluto, 28–30

R

Riddles, 49, 51, 52, 56, 58, 60, 62, 76, 77, 79, 83, 154, 156, 157

S

Schmitt, Harrison "Jack," 38–39
Scorpions, 54
Sheep, 55, 168
Sign language, 180–181
Space Station, International
life in the, 32–37
Olympic torch, 144
Squirrels, 54, 167
Strawberries, 78–83
Sword, Viking, 114

T

Table of Measures, 186
Temperatures, converting, 186
Toads, 55

V

Vampire bats, 165

W

Weather
Clouds, 40–45
Cold, 48–53
Plot symbols, 46
Proverbs, 54–55, 61
Week, origin of the, 20–22